WHAT I WANT MY KIDS (AND ME) TO KNOW:

Being Better Humans One Napkin at a Time

WHAT I WANT MY KIDS (AND ME) TO KNOW:

Being Better Humans One Napkin at a Time

By the Reverend Tyler Strange

South Carolina United Methodist Advocate Press

South Carolina United Methodist Advocate Press, Columbia, South Carolina

Copyright © 2024 by South Carolina United Methodist Advocate Press

Scripture quotations marked (NIV) are taken from The Holy Bible, New International Version, Copyright © 1973, 1978, 1984 by the International Bible Society. THE HOLY BIBLE, NEW INTERNATIONAL VERSION®, NIV® Copyright © 1973, 1978, 1984, 2011 by Biblica, Inc.® Used by permission. All rights reserved worldwide.

All rights reserved. No part of this book may be reproduced or transmitted in any form or by any means, electronic or mechanical, including photocopying, recording or by any information storage and retrieval system, without permission in writing from the Publisher.

First published in the United States of America in 2024
by the South Carolina United Methodist Advocate Press.

Library of Congress Cataloging-in-Publication Data
What I Want My Kids (And Me) To Know
p. cm.

Cover photos courtesy of Billion Photos (napkin) and ajphoto (marker).

ISBN 979-8-9883575-7-5

Dedication

For Lauren, Ava Grace, and Ellie Hope.
I can't believe we get to write this story together. Thank you.

Introduction

Connection, coaching, and spreading encouragement are my calling.

I feel fortunate to have found a vocation where I get to do this with wonderful human beings—most of whom already have a driver's license, are potty-trained, and put their dolls up before they spill cereal on said doll's dress.

But what about connecting and encouraging the tiny humans who call me "Daddy"?

I wasn't prepared for this adventure!

However, it's not just about connecting with our tiny humans; it is learning how to make meaning out of this beautiful invitation we all have to be human together.

We all want to be better humans and connect with our children.

We all want to be better humans and become better together.

What started as a daily lunchbox napkin to my daughter became an invitation for both to inspire one another to be better humans.

And in the process, inspire others.

In addition to the napkins, I began to write daily reflections for adults geared around similar themes of that day's napkin. Now, my daughter and I were partners in inspiring one another to be better humans.

What better way to win at home than to build a learning framework with our children?

Over time, I posted the napkins and corresponding reflections on social media. Not only did the napkins provide avenues for parents, teachers, and other childhood professionals to connect with their children, but the napkins began to meet adults in the tensions of their lives.

My friends began using the napkins to serve the children in their lives. They became conversation starters and whimsy whipper-uppers.

Not only were the napkins serving our daughter, but they were also serving us—her parents.

Through the power of a napkin, we have discovered a way to connect with our children, speak to the tensions and pain points of life, and, together with our children, create a movement that partners with our communities to move people in the direction of hope.

All because of a napkin.

—*Tyler Strange, April 2024*

1
Growing Up

I get sentimental on first days of school. It comes with the territory of raising little humans.

I remember when our oldest daughter began 4K at Ben Hazel Primary School in Hampton, South Carolina. This was no longer dropping her off for a few hours at Mother's Morning Out. This was a new beginning. She was growing up.

Growing up is a weird experience as a parent.

As my wife and I processed the moment in the car, our sadness began to dance with a new emerging feeling. A feeling that was new to us as parents.

A feeling that told us we were moving from one season of parenting into another.

> TIPS FOR STARTING 2nd GR:
>
> 1) No one sits alone at lunch.
>
> 2) Tell teachers "Thank you."
>
> 3) Rectangle pizza is a national treasure.
>
> We are cheering really loud for you!

It was a feeling of pride.

Although we felt unprepared for this moment, we realized our daughter was ready.

She was ready because part of our intention as parents has been to raise human beings who can do two things:

- Be present in the phase of life they are in; and
- Prepare to launch into the next phase of their life when it is time.

Now that I offered those pithy words of wisdom, can I let you in on the real secret to parenting?

The secret to parenting that no one tells you and you have to figure out on your own is this: No one knows what in the world we are doing!

We are all just taking our best guess. Every day is a collection of best guesses.

That's all. That is the secret of parenting. Take your best guess at hundreds of decisions each day and hope you don't choose the ones that will be the reason why your child needs therapy one day.

I say this in jest. Sort of.

Parenting is about a direction and a relationship. Every day we try to be intentional about parenting our children in a direction knowing that multiple paths can still lead in the same direction.

When the same oldest daughter of ours began second grade, I wrote a note of encouragement on a napkin and slid it into her lunchbox. It was an impulse move. I thought, "What would be a fun way to encourage our seven-year-old?"

Then I got to thinking—what would I go back and tell my seven-year-old self on the first day of second grade?

I can decisively say I would encourage seven-year-old Tyler not to take rectangular pizza for granted!

I'm curious. What would you add to this list?

What would you go back and encourage your second-grade self to do/be?

2
Habits

Habits form us and impact the world around us.

Individuals have habits. Communities have habits. Organizations have habits. Habits form culture and guide who we become.

Picking up a piece of trash instead of walking by it on a sidewalk is a habit. Making eye contact and saying "hi" when you walk by someone, instead of looking away, is a habit.

Seeing people is a habit.

Listening before speaking is a habit.

Being respectful and gracious is a habit.

Returning your shopping cart back to its designated location at the grocery store is a habit.

> IF YOU SEE TRASH, DO WHAT YOU CAN TO PICK IT UP.
>
> AND ALWAYS PUT YOUR GROCERY CART BACK AT THE GROCERY STORE!

A consistent commitment to the small things makes the big picture even more incredible.

The next generation is watching and taking their cues from us.

What are your habits building? What are your habits communicating?

3
Why Did It Take So Long?

I remember watching the 2021 presidential inauguration with my oldest daughter. After Vice President Kamala Harris's inauguration, I told my daughter this was the first time a woman had ever been vice president, let alone president, in our country's history.

Then my daughter asked, "Daddy, why did it take so long?"

She knew nothing about the embarrassing nature that has become modern politics in America.

What she saw at that moment was that it took more than two hundred years for a woman to hold this important office of leadership.

My five-year-old daughter said the quiet part out loud.

I am so glad she did.

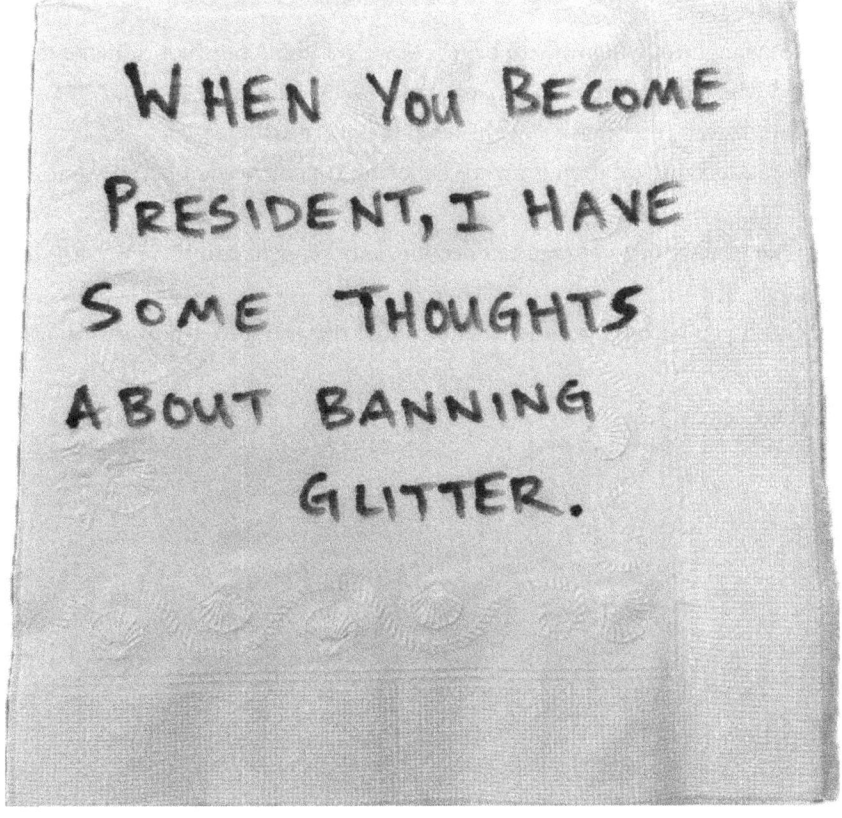

A big part of answering a call is discovering the courage to take the first step to follow that call.

We relate to story. When we see people—people who have chapters in their lives we can empathize and relate with—it inspires us to believe we can also do the thing they did, which changes worlds.

I know there are parts of your story that have the potential to inspire future generations.

Let's make it happen!

My daughters will grow up believing they can run for president if their gifts and passions take them in that direction.

My daughters will grow up believing they can start a nonprofit that meets society's most profound needs if their gifts and passions take them in that direction.

My daughters will grow up believing they can be pastors or principals or CEOs or coaches or teachers or builders or servers if their gifts and passions take them in that direction. It also doesn't hurt that we are fortunate enough to surround our girls with dynamic women who are already leaders in these vocations.

My daughters will grow up believing we are doing our best to make this a world where daughters don't have to ask, "Why did it take so long?"

But instead, they'll ask, "We're here. What's next?"

It matters our children grow up believing what is needed is also what is possible.

One generation's courage can become another generation's new path. It's possible.

But if you become president, I'm leading the anti-glitter movement!

4
The Path To School

When I taught high school, I learned never to assume every kid's trip from home to school and school back home is the same.

I remember one year, I had a student who slept every day during third block (middle of the day, around noon), and we butted heads all the time.

Finally, I asked him to stay after school one day so we could talk. He said he couldn't.

I asked, "Why?"

His answer taught me not only a valuable leadership lesson but a lesson about being human.

He said he had to be at work by 4 p.m.

Okay. A lot of students have after-school commitments. We can work

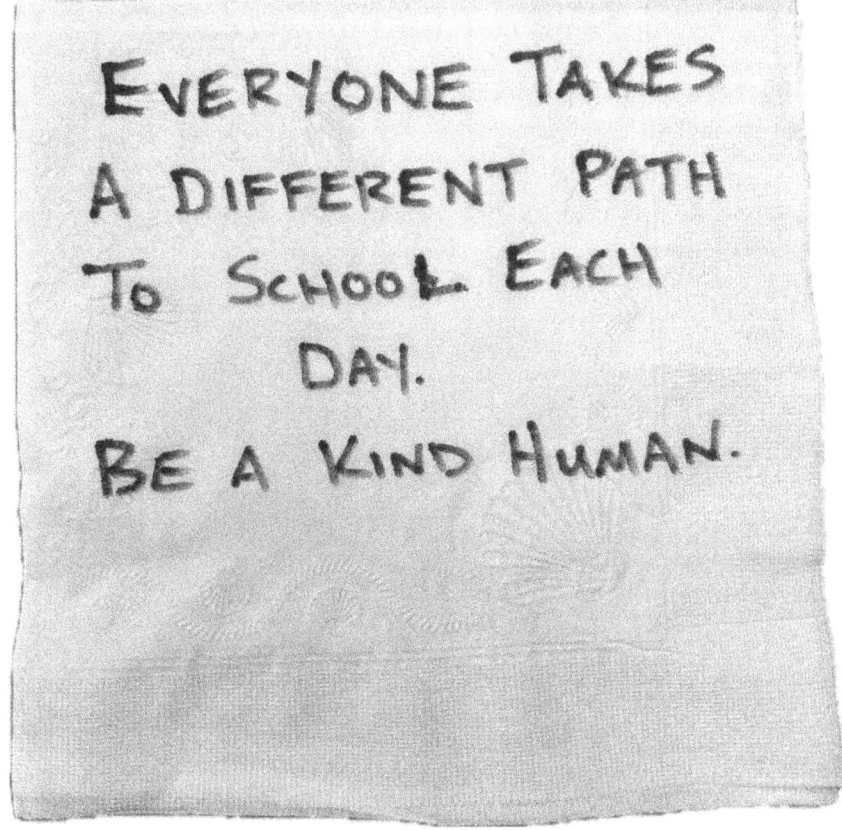

around those.

This young man worked from 4 p.m. to midnight.

Then he slept in his mom's car.

He didn't have access to a shower.

After sleeping in his mom's car, he would come to school every day.

Educators, mentors, and leaders learn quickly: Never assume we understand what the average kid has witnessed or experienced by the time they get to school.

This young man was sleeping in my class not because he was a lazy student but because he was doing all he could to support his family.

As a homeless seventeen-year-old.

I had a lot to learn about empathy and compassion and learning not everyone takes the same path to the same place.

It's presumptuous for anyone to say they understand someone if they don't know anything about their generational, geographical, or cultural context.

One of the best ways to get to know someone is to get to know their context. When we learn about context, we learn about the different paths people take to get to school, work, or church.

Be gracious and kind. Sometimes just showing up is massive.

Not all paths to where we gather are the same.

When we intentionally live with empathy and compassion to understand the paths we all take, we cultivate a healthy foundation for the future we want to make.

A future that levels the mountains and raises the valleys for as many people as possible.

Sometimes it just takes asking, "What is your morning like?"

5
Numbers

I love math. I love numbers.

I love data and the patterns it teaches us about life and human behavior.

I love that math is emotionally neutral.

There is a math joke I've heard countless times when people find out I have a math degree. You may have heard it. You may not have heard it. It goes:

There are three types of people in the world—those who like math and those who don't.

Think about the numbers in your life and what they can teach us. Or how the numbers can encourage us.

If we are willing to self-evaluate and dream a little, numbers help us create a direction and a process for wringing all we can out of life.

> ONE OF YOUR PARENTS ONCE TRIED TO CARRY TEN BAGS OF GROCERIES AT ONCE. ONE OF US LEARNED 9 BAGS WAS OUR LIMIT.
> WE ALSO LEARNED RANCH DRESSING ISN'T A SMELL THAT COMES OFF SHOES.

I have an app on my phone called "Parent Cue." This app provides daily cues to help us engage our children in age-appropriate conversations about faith and life. It also gives us a number. And that number tells a story.

Today, it told me we have five hundred and thirty-six weeks until our seven-year-old moves on to what is next. (Theoretically, "next" is graduating high school.) That seems like a lot of time—until it's not.

Every phase of a child's life is unique. As a parent, it feels like once we get our feet under us in one phase, it's time to launch our children into a new phase.

I still don't know how people write parenting books that aren't anything more than scratch-and-sniff group hugs for other parents living in the dog days of raising little humans.

Perhaps you have young children. Maybe your children are in high school, and that number of weeks until they move on to what is next is barreling down on you, and you're feeling all the feels while reading this. My bad.

Maybe your children are adults, and you understand childhood is just a phase and why we don't want to miss the opportunities unique to this stage. Please encourage us!

Or maybe you don't have any children you are legally responsible for, but thank God, you have children in your life who look up to you as a spiritual parent and call you "aunt," "uncle," or a name way more incredible than anything I can generate.

Numbers tell us the truth about reality. Numbers reveal what we value. Numbers remind us life moves in phases, seasons, and cycles.

Sometimes we know how long we have until our children, or we, have a "next." Other times, circumstances beyond our control dictate an earlier end to a phase than we either desired or anticipated.

It is no less significant whether a phase measures in hours, days, weeks, months, or years; it all matters.

Can we make our phases with each other count?

What numbers help you learn and grow?

6
Questions

I am interested in the questions we ask each other. Why? I have found inspiring people inspire us because of the questions they ask.

Think for a moment. How many times in the last day have you asked someone a question that broke the monotony of the day and invited them to show you a bit of what matters to them? Questions like:

What are you excited about?

Have you seen anything that inspires you?

What do you value?

Tell me what you have been thinking about lately.

In leadership, I pay attention to the questions, or lack of questions, people ask.

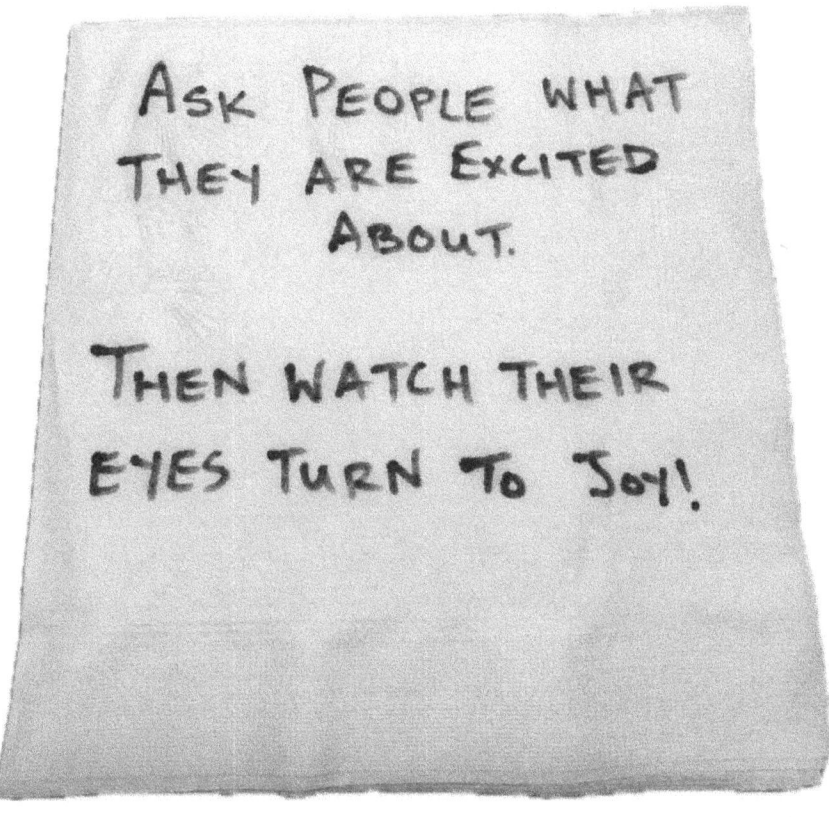

You would be amazed how many people are waiting to be asked these questions because they are surrounded by people who are self-absorbed or too emotionally immature to be aware of the possibility our shared humanity can generate.

People who ask inviting questions are people who make good friends and awesome sojourners.

And yeah, I'll say what we are all thinking. Who among us doesn't enjoy talking about themselves? Who among us doesn't like saying out loud something we may be excited about?

Good questions connect and inspire.

So today, try to learn something about the people you are with.

A good question can change everything.

7
We Can Do Hard Things

In the summer of 2020, our family went through a really difficult fifty-day stretch.

Our youngest daughter was born prematurely at thirty weeks and spent the first thirty-eight days of her life in the neonatal intensive care unit. As if there wasn't anything else going on in the world that summer, we found ourselves dropped into a storm we never saw coming.

I remember spending July 4 just like we did every day between June 28 and August 6, 2020: One parent would visit our daughter in the NICU while the other spent time keeping things as normal as possible for our oldest daughter at our friend's house, the house we called home for forty-six days that summer.

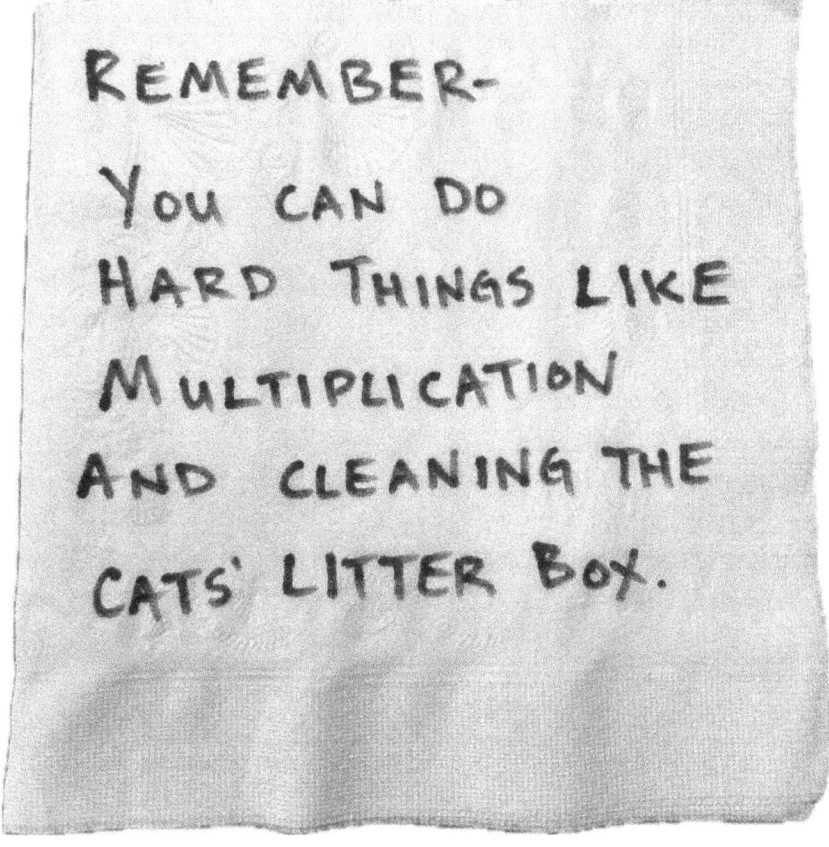

Seventy miles from our actual home in Hampton, South Carolina.

I remember having no idea it was even July 4 until we heard fireworks in the neighborhood that night.

That is kind of how the summer of 2020 felt for our family. Each day felt the same. One more day of getting our crew to the next day as healthy as possible until we got word the season was over.

We didn't know what day it was on the calendar. The only numbers we cared about were numbers measured in days, ounces, and milliliters.

When things sort of began to slow down and we were back home from our hospital stay—we lived in Hampton, South Carolina at the time and the hospital was in Augusta, Georgia—I remember one night asking our oldest daughter, "Did you learn anything from what our family went through?"

She responded, "Daddy, it was hard. But our family can do hard things."

Wow.

We made it through a really hard thing that summer.

The days (and nights—thanks, people who shoot fireworks at ungodly hours of the night) are long, but the years are short.

Progress happens one step a time.

Hope happens one choice at a time.

Both at the speed of love. Which moves at its own pace.

Hope is a direction, friends. I don't know who needs to be reminded of this today, but you can also do hard things.

It doesn't mean you resolve your anxieties and fears in one effort. What it means is that your next step is taken with the intent of walking in the direction of hope.

One step, one day, one breath at a time. Eventually, the small things add up and the big picture changes.

Things may stay hard for a while, but the way you navigate them doesn't take out your spirit.

You can do hard things when you make hope your direction. My seven-year-old and I believe in you.

8
Rhythms of Rest

Can we normalize healthy rhythms in life?

Can we start by modeling this to our children so they grow up believing "a good rest" is the standard and not something to be earned?

Yes, we want our kids to have the courage, willpower, and community support it often takes to feel like they can move mountains.

We also need to teach our children how to have the courage to recognize when their body is exhausted from everything required to move that mountain.

Then encourage them to know it's okay to stop "going."

It's okay to rest and take a break.

It's not a sign of weakness.

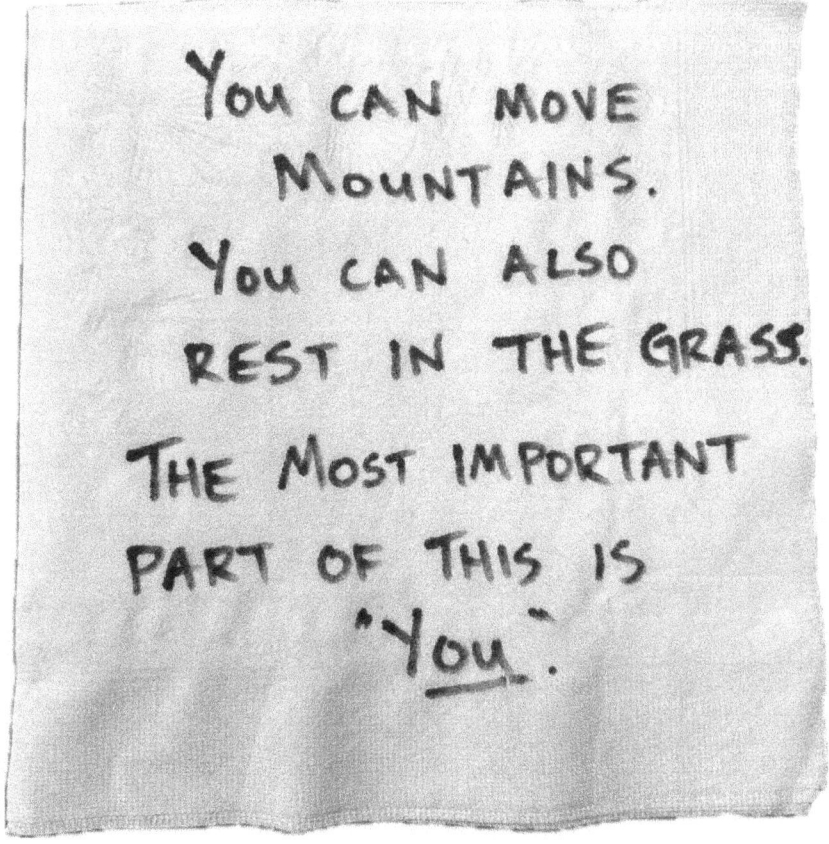

It's a sign of respect for the one body God gave you, and it's a mark of maturity to show that kind of discipline. Learning our limits and how to live within those limits is a sign of maturity.

When it's time to create and build ideas and things with our head, heart, and hands, be all in on that time.

When it's time to stop and rest, be all in on that time as well.

Can we start by normalizing healthy rhythms with, and for, our kids?

After all, we know more is caught than taught.

9
Baby Shark

What narratives do you tell yourself that aren't true?

Does a psychological wall arrive when you decide to start something new?

Do concrete boots form around your feet when you feel compelled to take a next step?

I'm too old.

I'm not educated enough.

I'm too out of shape.

What will they think? (There is always a "they," isn't there?)

I can't do _____.

Tell yourself the truth. You probably can be and do that thing/idea you have told yourself you couldn't do.

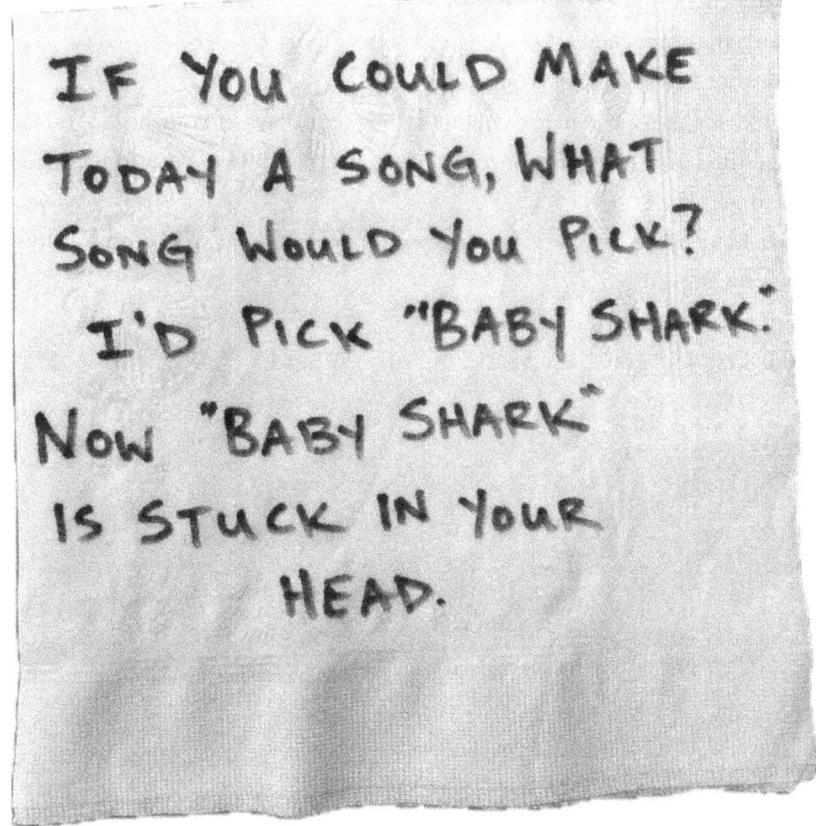

You just haven't because somewhere along the way you believed something about what you were capable of that wasn't true.

The narratives we listen to in our lives shape what we believe about ourselves and how we engage the world around us. My friends, I urge you to challenge those unhealthy narratives you believe about your life.

In his book *Soundtracks,* Jon Acuff suggests we ask three questions when it comes to assessing the narratives we believe about our life:

1. Is it true?
2. Is it helpful?
3. Is it kind?

What we believe ourselves can change. Can you take a small step toward changing any unhealthy narratives this week?

Schedule that appointment.

Increase your workout weight.

Go an extra two-tenths of a mile.

Schedule that first thirty-minute walk.

Write two hundred words.

Book that first class.

Ask that friend to keep you accountable.

You can change the negative soundtrack that plays in your head. You can change the narrative you believe about what is possible in your life. Change your song.

You have no idea what is waiting on the other side of who God is calling you to be and do.

I'm cheering for you!

But first, let's get "Baby Shark" out of your head.

10
The Inside-Out

I remember a difficult four-month stretch of life when everything I was responsible for was being disrupted. These weren't interruptions. They were disruptions.

An interruption is stubbing your toe. A disruption is dropping a brick on your toe then having your toe operated on and having to learn to walk a new way with a new center of balance.

The constant wave of disruptions left me physically, emotionally, and spiritually exhausted.

I remember telling my wife I needed someone I respected to tell me it was okay to take care of myself and let some plates fall to the ground.

I can't make this next part up.

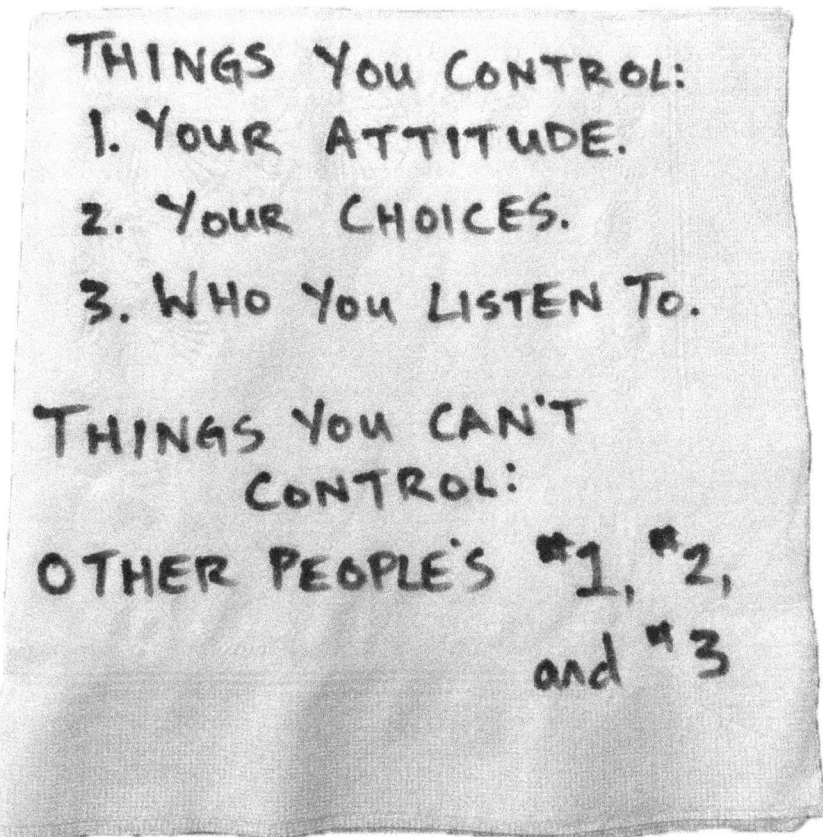

The very next day, I received an unexpected note in the mail from a respected clergy friend here in South Carolina. In the note, he encouraged me to live and lead from "the inside-out."

This invitation changed my life.

At the time, I was not aware of how much my identity, worth, and affirmation as a person was driven by how those outside my innermost circle received me.

Sure, there are elements to most jobs that involve assessment, affirmation, and how we relate to others. I get it. That is what it takes to build trust in business.

But I realized I had completely neglected the "inside" part of who I was and, instead, lived and led solely with how the "outside" would receive me.

This way of being is not healthy, nor is it sustainable.

If you need to hear this from someone else like I did in that season of life from my colleague, I encourage you to build your life from "the inside-out."

Here is your permission slip.

When you live from the inside-out, you become much more invested in the things you can control and the value this brings to your soul.

And when you have good soul care, you will always be surprised by how this naturally radiates "out."

You can do this, friends. Here is your invitation.

11
Listening

Listening makes so many things better.

It helps us to be present, to develop a healthy self-awareness.

And the most inspirational people I know are also the best listeners I know.

We can't connect with others if we don't listen, and we certainly can't learn from one another if we don't listen to one another.

What will you learn today that you didn't know yesterday? What do you want to learn to help you solve a problem your current knowledge base can't solve? Who do you need to spend time with over coffee to learn more about their perspective and help you understand where they are coming from?

Have you stopped to consider what is possible on the other side of your commitment to being a listening learner?

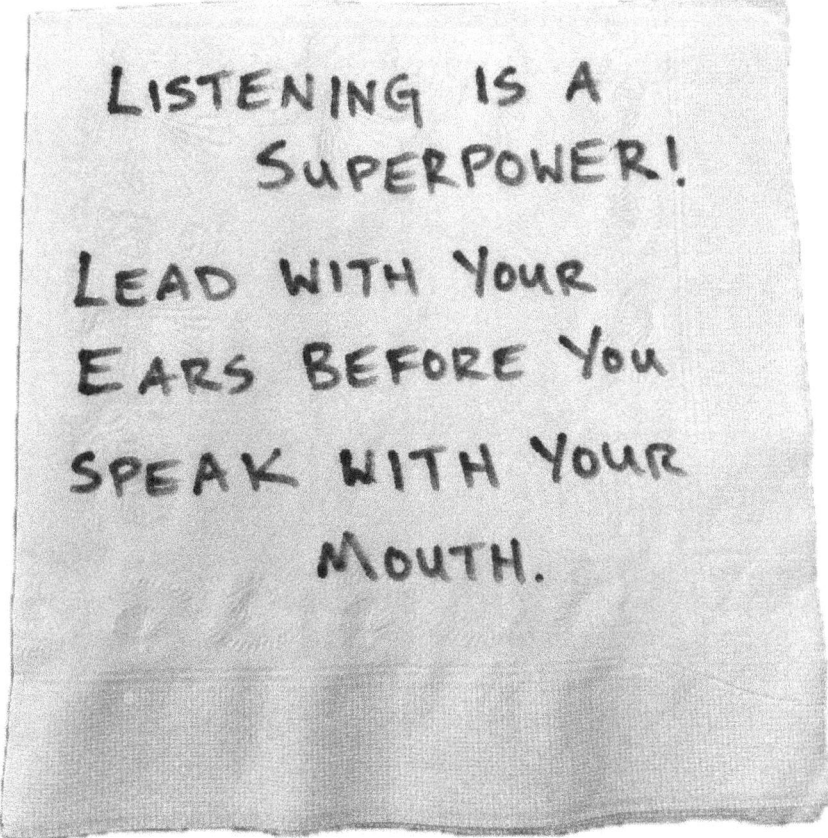

Your age and season of life is no match for the power of a curious mind.

You have the potential, right now, to learn something new today you didn't know yesterday.

Then, this something you learn today, it has the potential to make our tomorrow better.

The future belongs to those who are willing to listen and to learn—and to those who are willing to bring others into the learning with them.

And for those still in second grade, listening also helps us know when recess is!

12
Celebrate the Win

When my wife, Lauren, and I got engaged, we decided we would enjoy the process of our engagement season. Whenever we knocked something off our wedding to-do list, we would "celebrate the win" by toasting Mountain Dew poured in mason jars.

We were committed to making joy and celebration part of the season.

This taught us the value of creating a process we could stay engaged (pun intended) with while not allowing the pressure of the process (planning a wedding and a move at once) overwhelm the excitement of the journey.

I am often reminded that what we celebrate is what we repeat.

In the Christian scriptures, we see festivals as a time to remember the stories that formed them, celebrate the generational experiences that provide

wisdom, and share the values and lessons that frame the ethos of their culture. Celebrations pump life into cultures.

Today, celebrations remind us of what is good among us.

Celebrations create space for us to reflect and hear again the stories that remind us of our shared experiences and humanity.

Celebrations bring groups of people together.

Celebrations give us the chance to reaffirm and magnify those values we believe are essential to the quality of our communities.

Celebrations allow us to reaffirm the promises we have made in marriage, in parenthood, in friendship.

And, oh yeah—they are fun.

You shouldn't be embarrassed to celebrate someone or something good.

No Celebration Police will smack your wrist and say, "Hey, you! Stop celebrating the awesomeness of that person! It is uncalled for!"

No way.

Celebrations reinforce what is good in our world—community, relationships, and growth.

Lauren does this for our family on a weekly basis. She is always looking for people and events to celebrate. I love that about her. Her "celebration dedication" (I made that term up just now) is inspiring to me.

Celebrations are life-giving.

Can we have more parties? Can we fill the office with balloons? Can we turn on the karaoke? Can we order the cookie cake?

Celebrate!

What can you celebrate this week? Who can you celebrate this week?

13
Today

One of my favorite Winnie the Pooh scenes goes like this:

Pooh and Piglet are walking down a path and Pooh says to Piglet, "What day is it?"

Piglet squeaks, "It's today."

Pooh replies, "My favorite day."

We spend so much time dreaming about the future and what we want to happen that we neglect to remember that today is the tomorrow we dreamed about yesterday. Today is the culmination of the previous days. Tomorrow will have implications from what you do today.

What small habit can you start, change, or eliminate so the "tomorrow you" will be grateful for the "today you"?

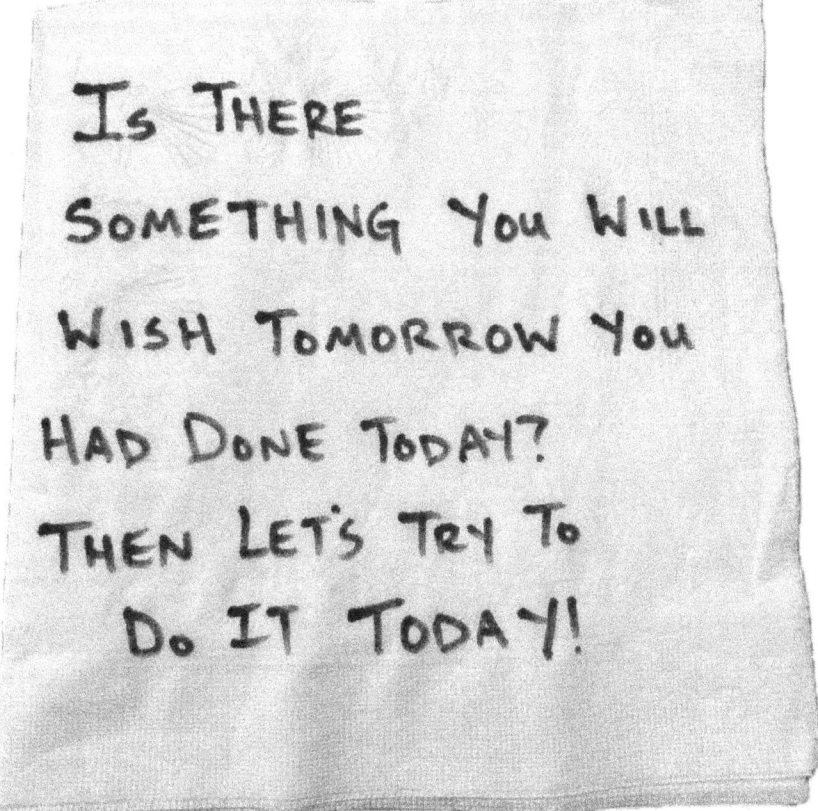

Is there something you will wish tomorrow you had done today? Then let's try to do it today!

Don't wait until tomorrow when you can start laying the foundation for that dream, that change, that new idea, or that act of kindness.

Today, make that call to connect with your people, make that appointment with a counselor, or talk with a mentor about your blind spots.

Today, buy the ingredients to finally attempt to make that entree you've been putting off because it seems intimidating. Do that thing today!

After all, today is the best day.

Your "tomorrow you" will thank you.

14
Don't Miss It

When it comes to raising children, no one tells you when you are doing something for the last time.

One day, we will pick our children up and hold them for the last time. We won't know it is the last time until we look back and realize we miss those moments.

One day we will play fort with our children for the last time in the living room. We won't know it is the last time until we look back and realize we miss those moments.

One day we will snuggle our children back to sleep after an oversight thunderstorm for the last time. We won't know it is the last time until we look back and realize we miss those moments.

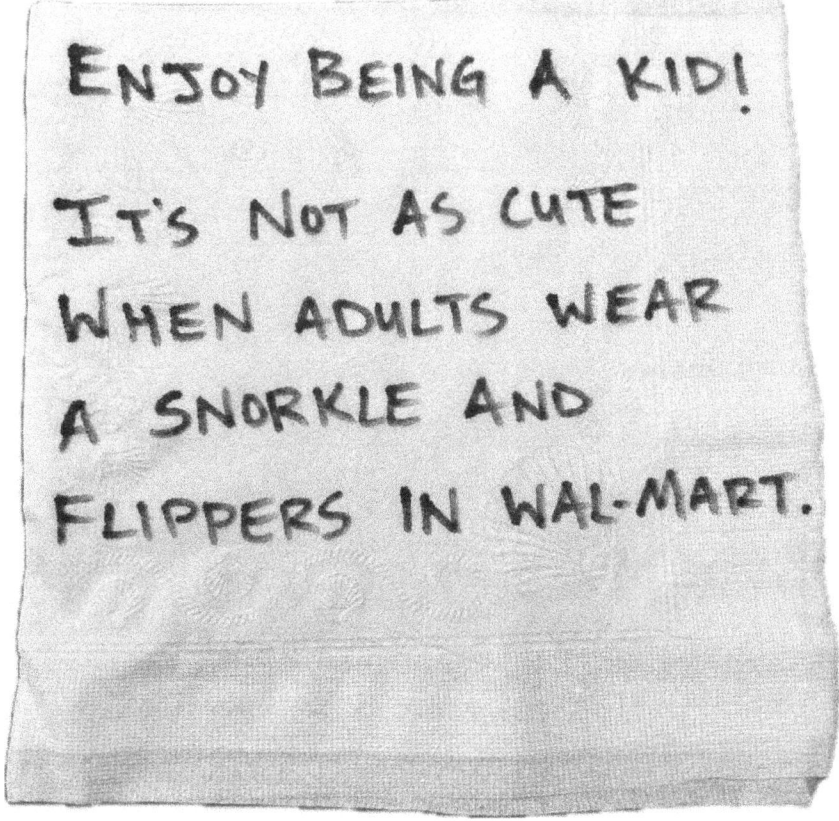

There comes a time when the innocence of wearing something fun is replaced by the concern for what others will think.

I struggle to embrace the mess.

And the chaos.

And the imagination that sometimes takes our beloved children into another world while I'm asking them multiple times to flush the toilet.

One day, I won't have to ask them to flush the toilet.

Because one day, we will realize we did something for the last time with our children.

The chaotic and the sweet. It all counts.

One day, the fun and innocence and wonder of childhood grows up. The days are long, but the years are short.

Our kids will have plenty of time to be adults.

I see you, mom and dad, grandma and grandpa. You're doing great.

Raising children is hard.

It is also a phase. Don't miss it.

15
Calling

Our calling is the way we are in the world. Our character is who we are with the world. To be called by God is to be invited into the deeper waters of God's work in the world.

Calling wrecks us.

Calling asks, "What is the way God is inviting me to be a vital part of the world?"

Calling is the drumbeat that sets the rhythm of the day.

If our days lack rhythm (not balance, rhythm—big difference), we probably lack a sense of call.

In my own life, my calling is coaching and teaching for transformation.

Leaving each season of my adult life has been challenging because we have been in beautiful communities with wonderful people each time. Still, growth and maturity could only happen with a new expression of my calling.

Remember that responding to God's call has the potential to transform not only the individual but also the networks where we live and work.

Frederick Buechner wrote, "The place God calls you to is the place where your deep gladness and the world's deep hunger meet."

So you be you. God has uniquely called you to be you.

And if you try to be anyone other than you, we're all missing out.

16
The Way Makes the Way

Robert Frost wrote, "Way leads to way."

"Way leads to the way" is the framework for how my values guide my steps and order my day.

What does this mean?

Consider this: Everybody has at least one paradigm-shifting idea the world needs. That idea often doesn't even see the light of day, let alone the discernment of a process, because most people fear their idea will not resonate with other people.

Share your idea with someone.

Don't paralyze yourself by thinking about the end game. This will reveal itself at the right time.

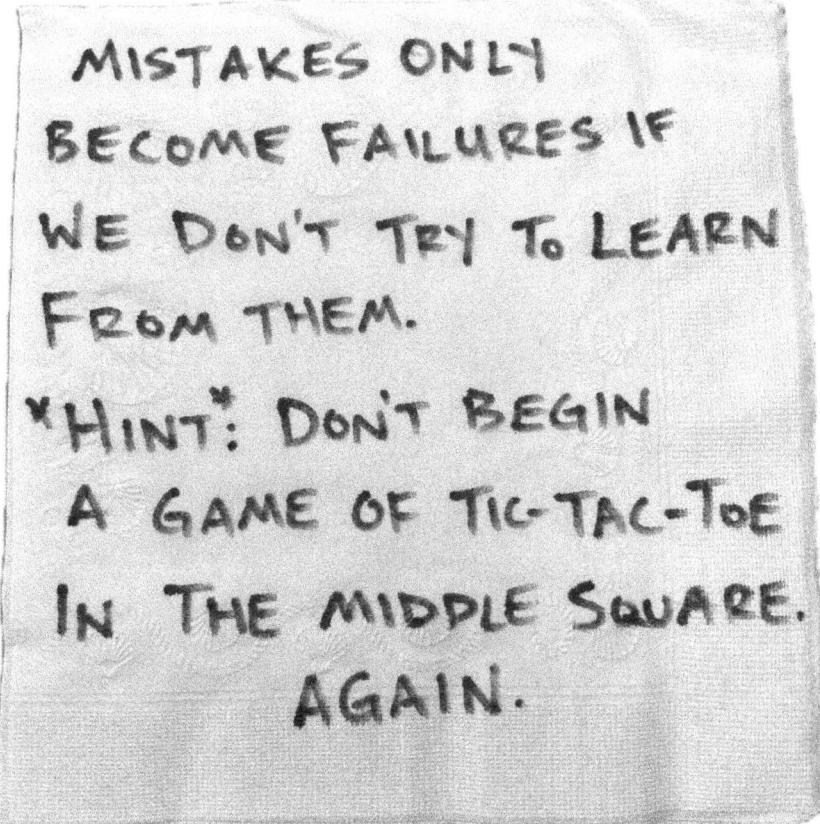

Take the first step.

Do something, anything, to start your idea.

You can't make the way if you don't start walking.

Remember, way makes the way.

What is that call you have burning inside of you? Tell someone.

Take small steps to engage the call.

Look for ways to follow the breadcrumbs of the call while you are in your current season.

But most importantly, don't be afraid to make a mistake.

I love learning. The learning process is why the idea of making a mistake doesn't terrify me. Making a mistake means I am closer to learning something new.

"Way makes the way" means the lessons we learn from our mistakes can become stepping stones to a new way—a way we create.

The first "way"—our choices, victories, struggles, learnings, etc.—makes the second "way"—path and direction.

The way makes the way.

17
Crockpot Life

With a nod to the ninety-nine-cent G&W frozen pizzas that filled our freezer in college, meals in a crockpot often have something meals we zap in a microwave do not—flavor.

Life isn't much different than meal prep.

A crockpot life often has more flavor than a microwave life.

Be someone whose life becomes a stew in a crockpot, not a series of TV dinners cooked in the microwave.

There is value in taking however long it takes for the gifts in our lives to mature and bring the flavor of our hearts to the work of our life.

To cut corners is to bring something out of the crockpot before it's ready.

We tell our daughter, "No one jumps to center stage from the backseat of

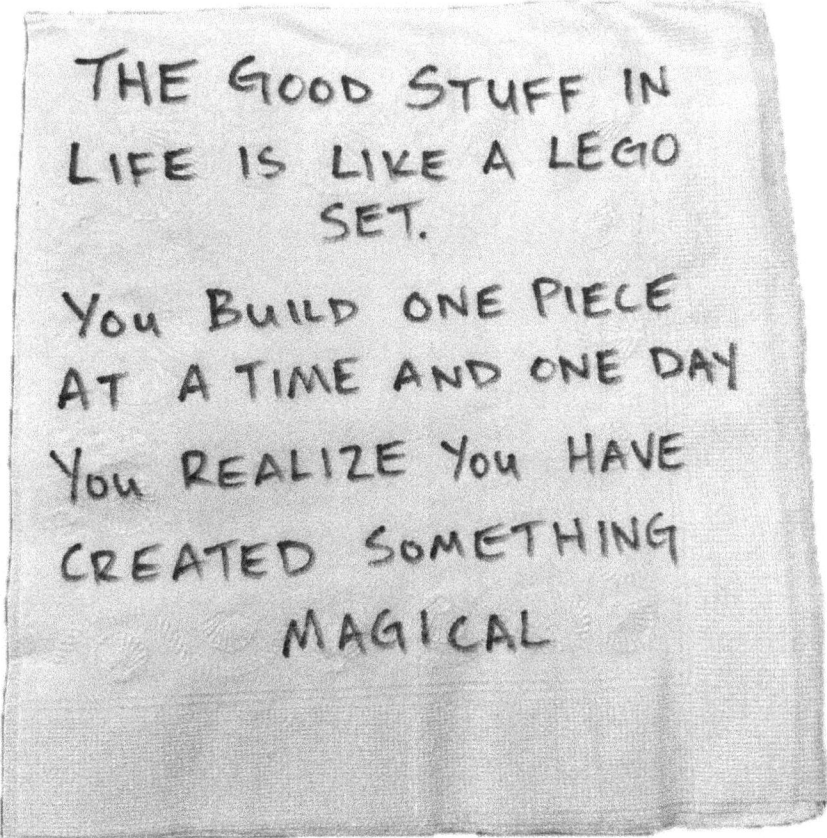

the car. You have to take the stairs to the stage."

When you cook with a crockpot, you can turn the heat up or down when necessary. If you rush a crockpot meal, well, you're probably left needing to default to a microwave meal. And no one wants that!

But in this day and age of "What have you done for me lately?," we cannot compare the start of our journeys with the middle of someone else's.

Something cooked in a crockpot has so much more quality to it than something
cooked in a microwave.

Life is better in the crockpot than in the microwave.

Sixty-year-old you will thank you for this.

Ninety-year-old you will love you for this.

Your dearest friends will want to travel through life with you.

And future generations will enjoy sitting under the shade of the trees created by your life's work.

Crockpots are better than microwaves.

18
Michael Jordan

I enjoyed the docuseries *The Last Dance* when it debuted on ESPN in 2020. *The Last Dance* told the story of the 1997-1998 Chicago Bulls National Basketball Association championship team.

I remember watching this team as an eighth-grader and wishing the Indiana Pacers and Utah Jazz could keep them from their sixth championship in eight years.

We don't like winners unless they are our winners.

As I watched the final episodes in the series, I was captivated by how Michael Jordan described the last minute of the deciding sixth game.

Jordan scored the Bulls' last six points in a final minute that saw the Bulls come back from an 83-81 deficit to win 87-86. Jordan's effort included a

> LONG BEFORE HE SAVED THE UNIVERSE IN SPACE JAM, MICHAEL JORDAN WAS CUT FROM HIS HIGH SCHOOL BASKETBALL TEAM. BUGS BUNNY IS GLAD MICHAEL DIDN'T GIVE UP!

game-changing steal with twenty seconds left, leading to his championship-winning shot.

Hearing Jordan talk about this final minute and how he processed playing in pressure environments is something that will stay with me for a while.

Jordan said, "How can I worry about a shot I have yet to take?"

Jordan was known for his ability to be fully present in a moment on the basketball court.

What does that mean? It means he didn't worry about missing a shot. He played free. He embraced the moment for all it could be.

Why did he not worry about missing a shot?

"How can I worry about a shot I have yet to take?"

Toward the end of *The Last Dance*, there is a scene where Jordan is celebrating the Bulls championship by pretending to play the piano in his hotel room. (Yes, Jordan had a real piano in his hotel room.) A reporter asks him about the future of the Bulls dynasty.

Jordan's reply? "Come on, man. It's the moment. It's the moment. You've got to get in the moment and stay here. Just stay in the moment."

Don't let a shot you have yet to take rob you of the opportunity to be fully present in the moment God has placed before you today.

Take the shot when it's time.

But until then, don't worry about a shot you have yet to take.

19
1979

Christian author Dr. Henry Cloud shares a story from a conversation he had with one of the best professional golfers of all time, Jack Nicklaus.

Cloud said he approached Nicklaus and asked, "Did you ever make significant changes to your golf swing?"

Nicklaus started laughing.

He then said, "I read about these guys. They get a new teacher and change (their swing). No, I never changed my swing."

Nicklaus continued, "The worst year I ever had, I don't think I won a tournament."

In 1979, Nicklaus suffered a lapse of form and did not win a tournament.

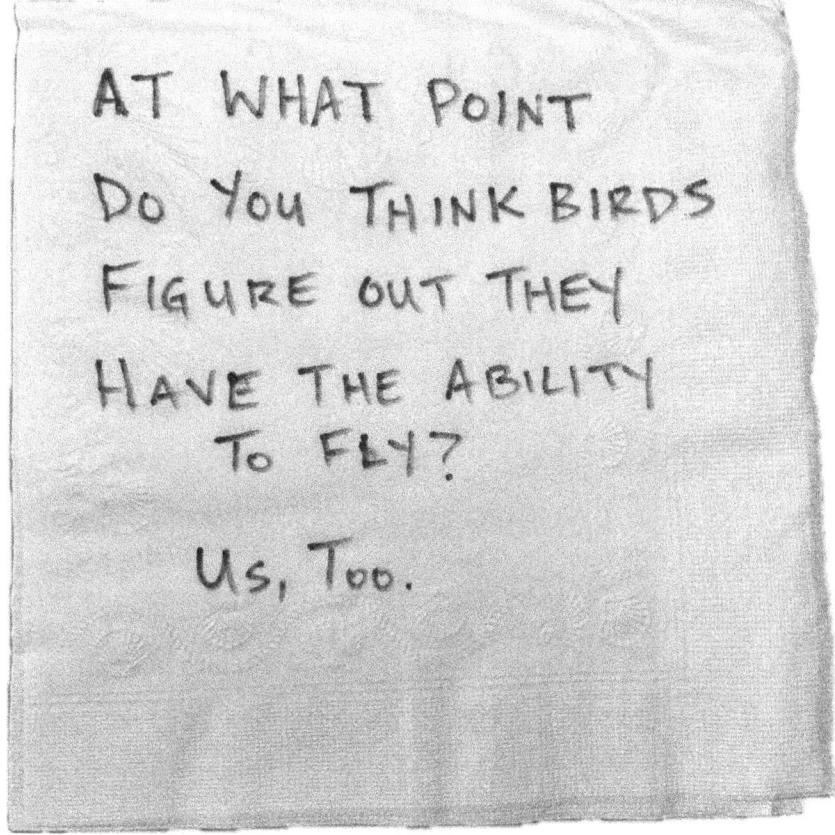

1979 was the first year in his professional career in which he failed to win a PGA Tour event.

Do you know what he did?

He returned to his childhood coach, Jack Grout, and said, "Teach me the game again."

Nicklaus is arguably one of the top three golfers of all time. Yet he still returned to his coach and said, "Teach me again."

He continued, "Let's start with the grip, and then I want to go to the stance. And he went back to those fundamentals that grounded me."

Do you know what happened the next year, in 1980?

He won two major golf tournaments.

In total, Jack Nicklaus won eighteen majors in his career. The next closest is Tiger Woods with fifteen majors.

When things started to feel like they were going in the wrong direction, Nicklaus didn't try to cut corners or find a silver bullet. Nicklaus got back to the basics.

Nicklaus knew the fundamentals that made up the essence of his golf swing.

What fundamentals do you need to be aware of that make up the essence of who you are?

20
Yes and No

We've heard, "Let your 'yes' be 'yes' and your 'no' be 'no.'"

Honoring our decisions is one trait I repeatedly notice as a separator between people with influence and people without influence.

Why? Trust.

When we show a pattern of "yes" means "yes" and "no" means "no," it builds trust.

Guess what trust produces? Influence.

Consider job titles, authority roles, teachers, parents, and friendships. All have significant potential—positive and negative—for profound influence because they put us in proximity to people.

Whether that influence takes root has to do with trust.

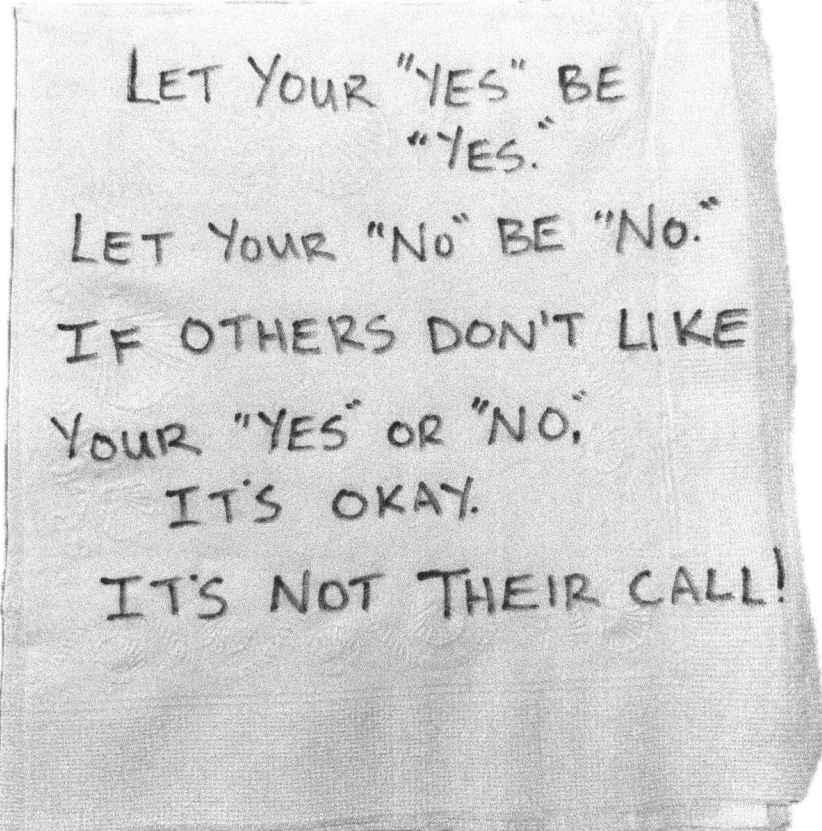

Do you know what else a commitment to honoring your yeses and noes creates?

Boundaries.

Healthy boundaries create healthy lives.

When you respect the boundaries you need to be healthy, others respect you more.

You have one life. One body. One family. You have one shot at creating and living a meaningful life.

Embrace the responsibility of owning your decisions.

Let your "yes" be "yes" and your "no" be "no."

Trust and boundaries are two things that signify, when we have them, that we are healthy, and, when we lose them, that we ache.

We need the best you in this world. No one else knows what decisions this requires more than you.

Thank you for taking care of yourself.

21
Read

Leaders are readers. Readers are learners. Learners make the world a better place.

Think about everything we gain from making reading a daily habit and everything we lose when we don't.

A habit of reading from a variety of authors with a diversity of backgrounds is a commitment to being a better human.

Reading keeps our minds fresh.

Reading expands our worldview and offers us perspectives we might not otherwise discover if left to our echo chambers.

Reading creates opportunities to form conversations with old and new friends.

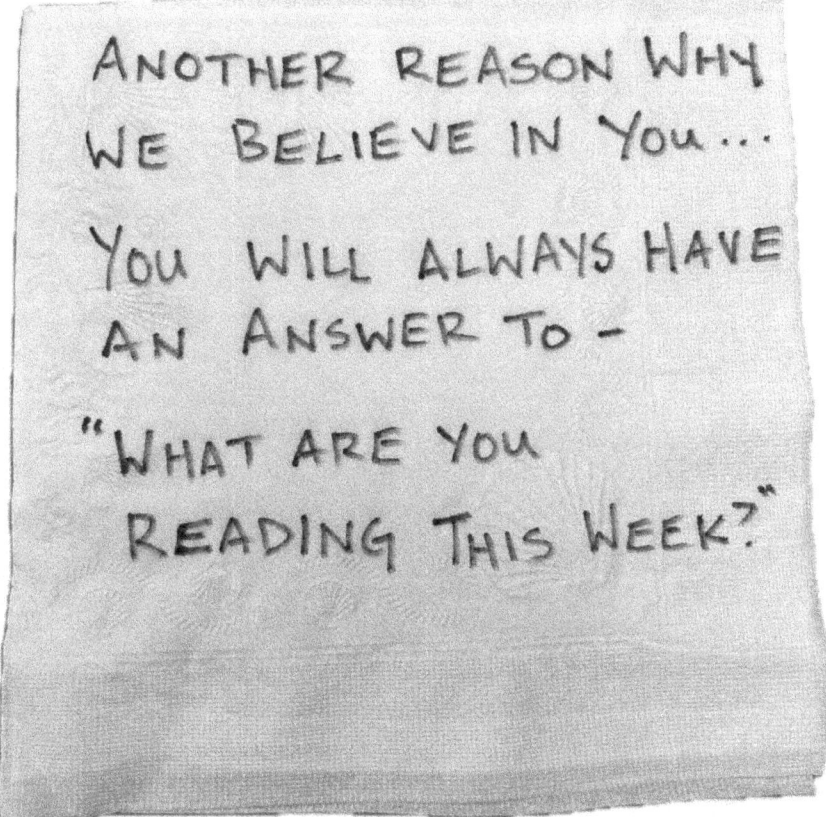

Reading is like food. If you put unhealthy junk in your body, it will have an unhealthy effect on your life.

If you are intentional about developing a healthy reading habit, it will have a healthy effect on your life and relationships.

Reading cures ignorance, develops empathy, and reminds us of all we still have to learn.

One question I like to ask leaders is, "What are you reading right now?" This answer, or lack of an answer, often tells me how committed an individual is to owning their development and growth.

How does reading affect your development? If reading a physical book is a challenge, try audiobooks. I've "read" as many audiobooks in the last four years as physical books.

It all counts. Just start.

22
Punch-Out

In golf, sometimes the golf ball doesn't go where you want it to go.

Hitting shots from off the beaten path happens more frequently for some of us than it does for others.

And sometimes, when the golf ball goes off-line, it rests in a spot that can make the next shot more uncomfortable than a ball in the middle of the fairway.

Life isn't much different.

Sometimes the wind blows, and our life is in a season we didn't plan on encountering. Sometimes life puts a tree between us and the target.

I once played golf with a man in his late eighties. His score was considerably higher than his age, but when you have played golf as long as he has,

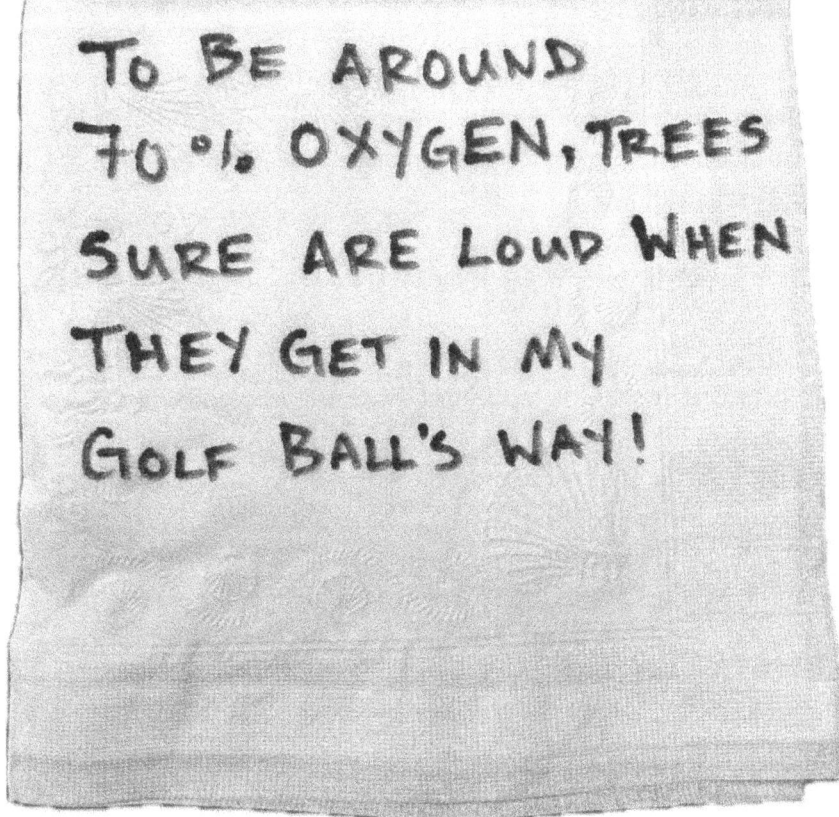

TO BE AROUND 70% OXYGEN, TREES SURE ARE LOUD WHEN THEY GET IN MY GOLF BALL'S WAY!

the company is way more interesting than the golf (I hope this is true of me!).

This gentleman's shot had come to rest about twenty yards behind a tree.

He could take his medicine, hit a shot sideways into the fairway (a "punch-out"), keep his score manageable, and get on to the next hole with minimal damage.

Or ... he could try to hit a difficult shot curved around a tree and onto the green. We call this the "hero shot."

He decides to try the hero shot.

His reasoning is, "At my age, no one cares if I save bogey. The better story is to go for this shot!"

His ball hit the tree and kicked back to our feet.

Without missing a beat, he turns to me and says, "And they say trees are seventy percent air."

I couldn't stop laughing while he made a mess of the hole, and ultimately his round, for the next fifteen minutes.

The point is that, sometimes, the punch-out is okay.

In golf, how we respond to the next shot depends on the tools in our tool kit. I may not have the same physical tools a PGA professional has to go around the tree. However, the tools I have may support a punch-out into the fairway and still keep my overall score in a good direction.

Ships change course.

Planes adjust flight plans.

These punch-outs don't change the overall direction; they create a different path.

Yes, trees are indeed made up predominantly of air. But sometimes in life, it's okay to swallow our pride, make wise decisions, and do what is necessary to get to the next step, the next day, and the next opportunity while preserving the integrity of our process.

Punch-outs rarely feel heroic.

Disciplined living and mission-driven decision-making in the face of adversity rarely feel exciting. Yet when we look back on the process, the excitement is in the experience of building something worthwhile.

Punch-outs are part of the process. Keep building, my friends.

23
Deep Breath

Deep breaths are one of the best things we can do for our bodies.

In a session with my counselor a few years ago, she explained most people get deep breathing wrong.

"How so?" I inquired.

She said most people tend to believe the checkpoint for a good deep breath is to notice our lungs.

Makes sense. I mean, lungs and breathing kind of go hand in hand. But when we focus on our lungs, we often exaggerate a shoulder shrug to convince us we are breathing deeply.

She suggested I try a different focus for deep breathing. Instead, place my hand on my stomach and force a deep breath that engages my stomach.

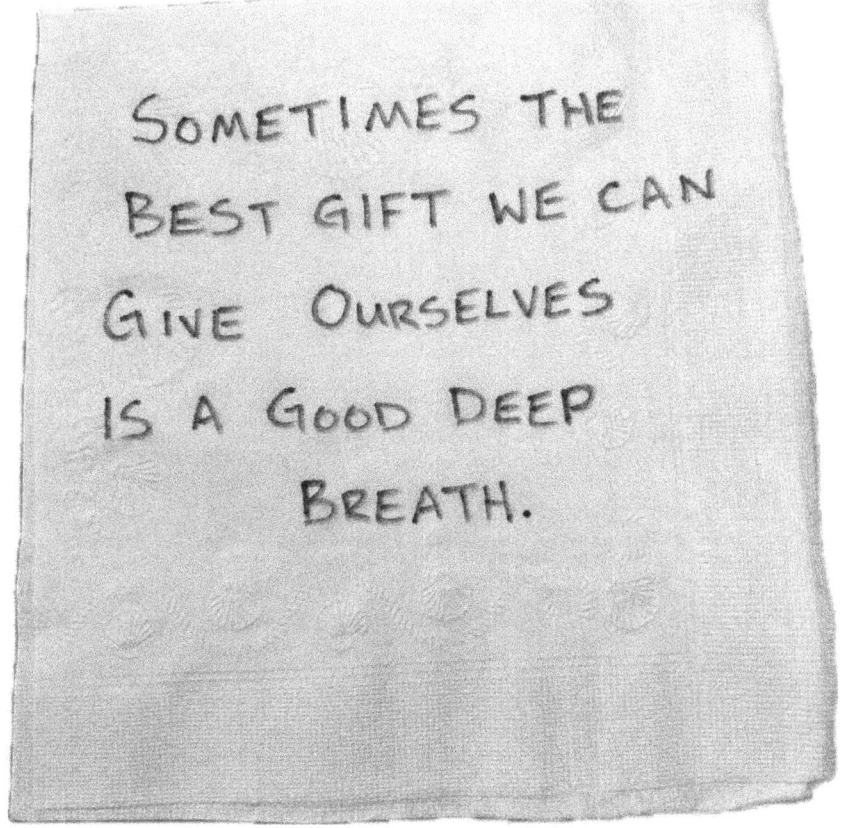

It's not a deep breath unless you feel your stomach inhale and exhale in sync with your mouth.

Deep breathing from my stomach changed so much about how I triage stress and anxiety when it shows up. A deep breath that engages the stomach will reset your nerve impulses at that moment and relax your body.

Exaggerate the feeling of your stomach going up and down. That's a natural deep breath.

Deep breaths from the stomach give us a chance to reset and free up our bodies. Deep breaths are one of the best ways to reset our bodies in moments of stress and anxiety.

Try giving yourself, at minimum, four thirty-second windows during the day to focus on deep breathing in your stomach and see what happens to your body.

Wait!

Before you turn the page, take an intentional deep breath now. How did that feel?

24
Superheroes

I think a lot about the genealogy of courage.

I'm a Batman fan. Batman doesn't need power from another planet or mythological genetics to do what he does.

But we also know it's easier to write a fictional story that includes courageous praxis than live a nonfiction life where courage happens in reality.

Courage is hard.

Without looking it up, how would you define courage?

Courage is answering a call when there is fear, uncertainty, or anxiety. That is my definition of courage.

Too many good ideas and gifted people stay stuck outside the arena because they never dared to step into the arena and courageously carry forward

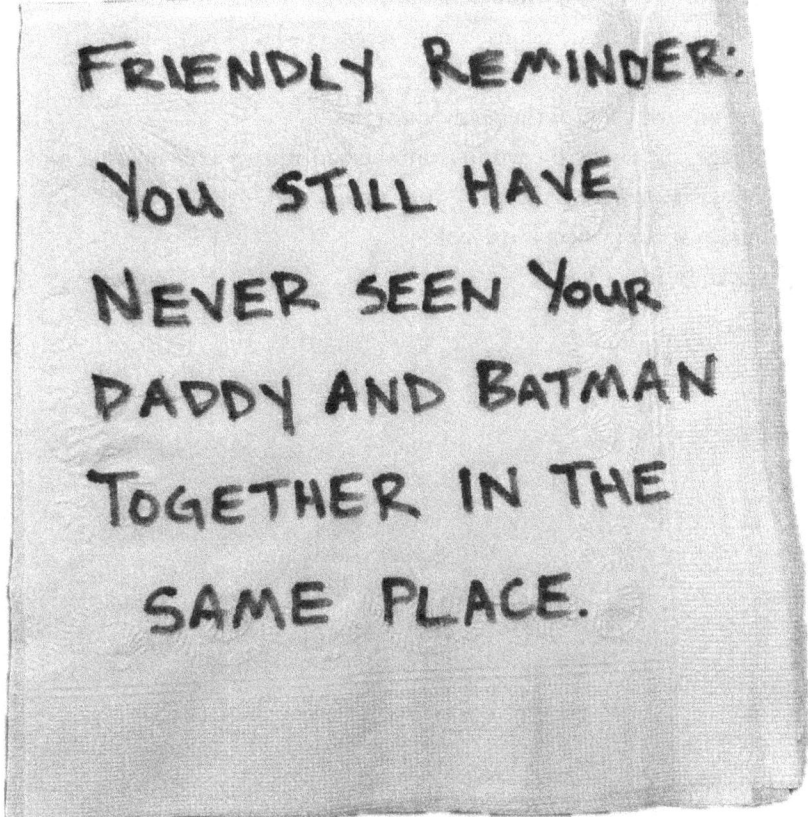

their great idea or launch the next movement that can transform their community.

Courage launches us from comfort into discomfort.

Courage launches from a place of obedience.

You prepare for courage.

I don't need the courage to be the guy who replaces Garth Brooks. Nothing in my life up to this point suggests any acumen or obedience that would make being a lead singer of a popular world tour something I would need to explore seriously. I would need to learn how to sing first.

Courage needs community to discern next steps and be the voice of support when fear tries to keep us from growing and offering our gifts to the world.

Author Brené Brown once said, "You can choose courage, or you can choose comfort, but you cannot choose both. They are mutually exclusive. Comfort is something you chase. Courage is something you choose."

Courage isn't just for fictional characters.

I see courage every day in parents of young children, in older adults who dare to make healthy decisions, and in teachers who show up every day to serve our children.

These are just a few of the many examples.

Courage isn't saving the world from the bad guys in a blockbuster movie.

Courage is answering the call—your unique call.

Courage is everywhere if we look.

It's even inside of you.

25
The Good Ole Days

The "good ole days" holds a nostalgic place in the hearts of many. We romanticize the "good" of the good ole days.

When I think of the good ole days, my mind immediately goes to the ball field my friend Michael and I created in our neighborhood.

My brother had a friend whose family owned a little gift shop that sat on the corner of Tigerville Road and Enoree Road in Travelers Rest, South Carolina. For two summers, until we outgrew the dimensions and weren't interested in transitioning to Wiffle ball, this field became our Sandlot—our little Field of Dreams.

First base was the propane tank. If you threw the ball and hit the tank before the runner got there, they were out.

Third base was a fence pole that guarded the side of Michael's grandparent's house.

The drainage ditch behind home plate caught unhittable pitches, and you weren't allowed to use any new bats.

During these summers, the Easton Hammer baseball bat became iconic to our little group of ballplayers in Travelers Rest.

Our group from our Travelers Rest Sandlot could hold our own. A Major League Baseball organization eventually drafted two of the guys who played in our sandlot. Two more played college baseball. One became a pastor.

We did all right.

These were the good ole days before opportunity took us all from the Sandlot to fields and stadiums that were well-manicured and had crowds.

Although, if asked, we might all still argue that propane tanks make better bases.

Then something happened.

We played at the Sandlot for the last time.

No one knew it was the last time when it happened. It just happened. The good days became the good ole days.

In the series finale of *The Office*, the character Andy Bernard said the following: "The weird thing is now I'm exactly where I want to be. I've got my dream job at Cornell, and I'm still just thinking about my old pals. Only now they're the ones I made (at my old job). I wish there were a way to know you're in the good ole days before you've actually left them."

While we leave the good ole days behind, we never leave what made them good.

Remember what made the good ole days good. Now go and make some good new days.

But no propane tanks are allowed—unless someone grills at the tailgate.

26
Drake

AJ called me the "Preacher Coach."

I knew him as an outstanding basketball player who would frustrate me with some immature decisions. But we got along fine.

Following a day of games at the state tournament, we were at a team meal, and I noticed AJ was eating by himself. He had his headphones on while he ate, and I reminded him we don't wear headphones at team meals.

Then I got curious and asked him why he wore his headphones everywhere.

He told me so he wouldn't have to talk to anyone.

I responded, "You mean like I'm doing right now?"

He cracked a smile. "Yeah."

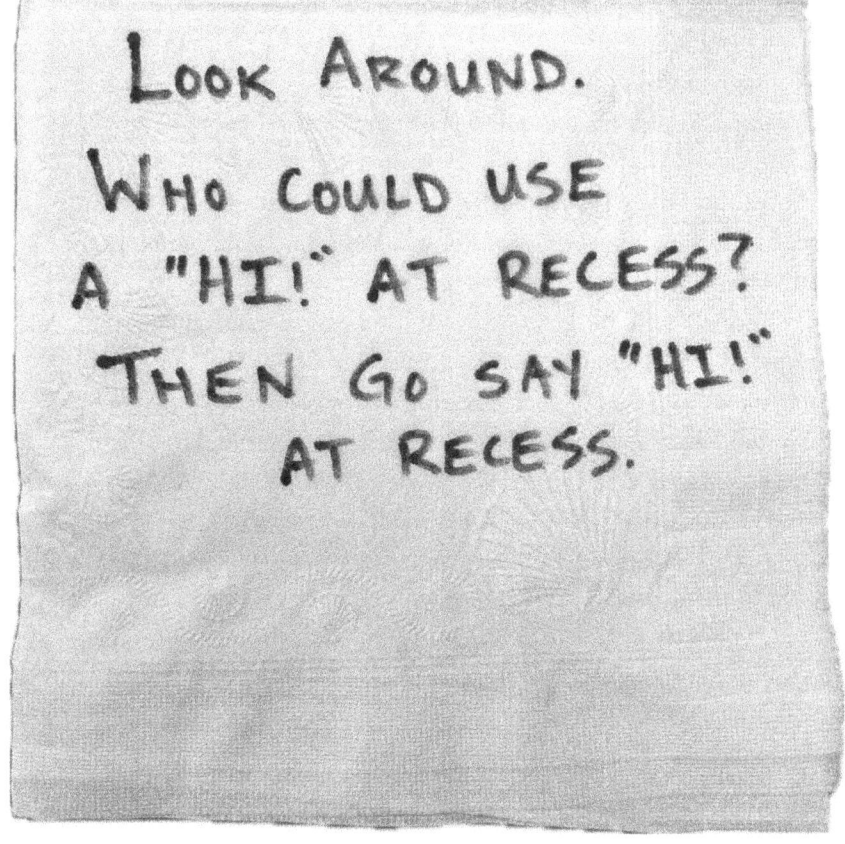

I asked him what he was listening to, and he said, "Early Drake." (Ask your grandkids.)

Then I asked him what drew him to Drake.

I like hip-hop and wanted to hear why he did. We had a good conversation. But it felt like there was more to learn about what made AJ tick.

A couple of days later, we met for breakfast. I wanted to get to know AJ better.

AJ told me he stopped going to high school during his sophomore year because he couldn't consistently attend school given his family situation. He was a sophomore academically but eighteen in age.

He struggled to get to school because he lived in four different places during his sophomore year while his mom worked two jobs (thirty-five minutes apart) to take care of his family.

There was more.

AJ's father died when he was nine of a drug overdose. He watched his dad eat cocaine when law enforcement arrived on the scene.

AJ would grow up and probably not see his thirties, just like every other male in his life.

Just like his dad.

I learned AJ didn't want that. But he didn't know how to be anything else.

At that point in AJ's life, playing basketball was the only time people cared about him. Now he was out of school with no stable community around him.

AJ just needed to be seen. He needed someone to care about AJ, the human, not AJ, the basketball player.

He took the chance to share his story when asked.

He had never been asked, "What happened in your life?"

Instead, he was constantly asked, "What is wrong with you?"

Today, rather than giving someone you don't know a judgmental stare and thinking to yourself, "What is wrong with you?," stop, see them, and say "hi." Discover what matters to them.

Everything changes when we see people as someone who matters to God instead of a problem we need to fix.

27
Streetlights

Robert Louis Stevenson, the author of classic books like *Treasure Island*, spent his childhood in Edinburgh, Scotland, in the nineteenth century.

As a boy, Stevenson was intrigued by the work of the old lamplighters who went around with ladders and torches setting streetlights for the night.

One evening, as young Robert watched with fascination, his parents asked him, "Robert, what in the world are you looking at out there?"

With great excitement, he exclaimed, "Look at that man! He's punching holes in the darkness!"

I know there is still plenty of good around us.

I know the number of people willing to punch holes in the darkness far exceeds the number of people who want to keep the lights out for the neighbors.

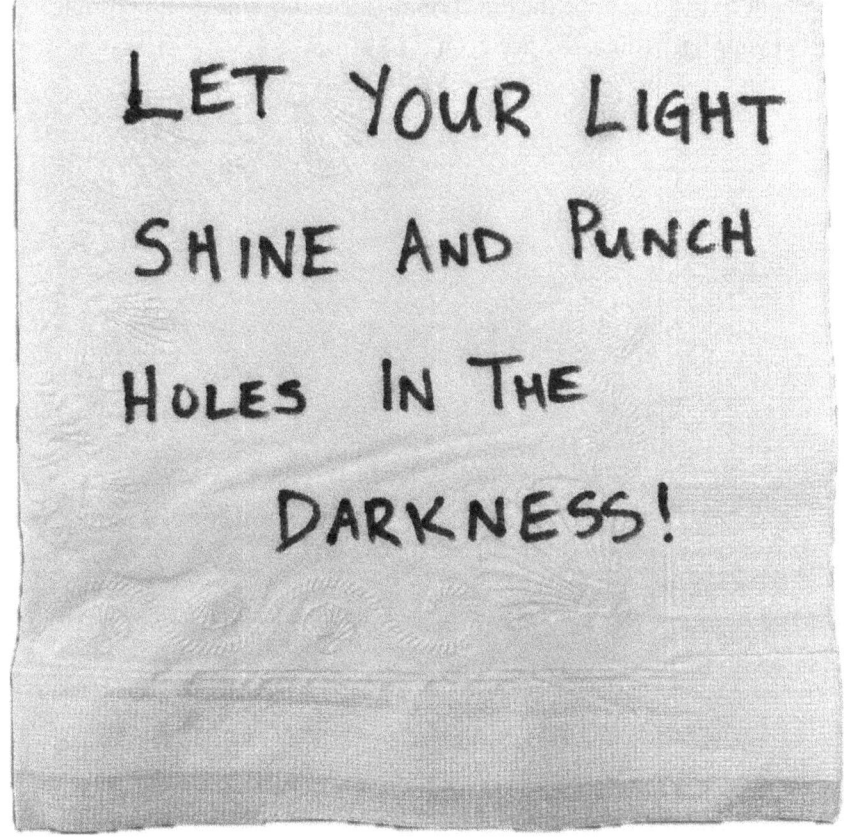

When we set out to punch one hole in the darkness, others have a way of joining us on the journey.

Light has this unique power to draw us in.

What do lights do when you get closer to them? They get brighter and warmer.

Streetlights, night-lights, and floodlights give light to the dark places in our communities.

You never know who will be inspired by your commitment to punching holes in the darkness.

Be a kind human.

Replace fear-mongering with hope-dealing.

Counter division with conversation and curiosity.

Squeeze out the dark by multiplying the light.

Turn walls into tables and obstacles into bridges.

Punch holes in the darkness.

You never know who is watching and who will be inspired by your commitment to making hope the direction in our communities. It's possible.

Let your light shine. We need you.

28
Check Engine

So I'm wondering, how are you doing? Like, really?

When people ask me that now, I feel like this question has never been more complicated to answer in my whole life.

When I get asked "How are you doing," I pause, hesitate, and then all these thoughts go through my mind.

"Should I tell you the truth?"

"Are they just being courteous and don't want a complex answer?"

"Or should I answer it contextually, like how am I doing based on what is going on that week?"

I bail out and usually say, "I'm good."

How are you doing? It's a complicated question to answer.

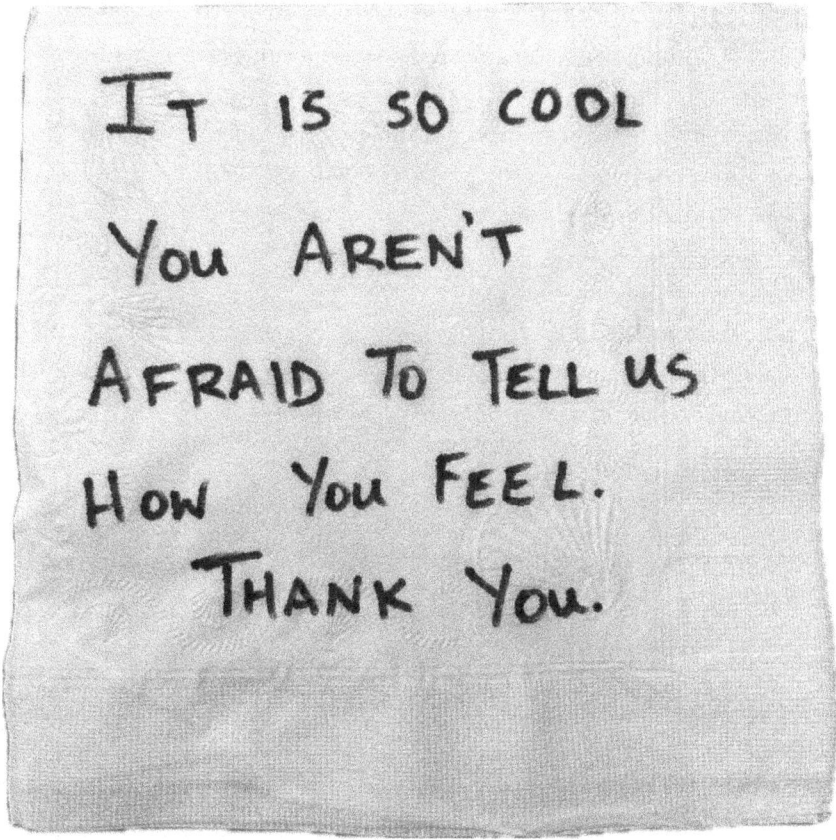

However, this is an important question we must ask ourselves, and it is a question we must be honest in answering.

Caring for our emotional health must also extend to our children.

We teach them to be aware of physical, spiritual, and relational health.

If being an adult human who spends time with other adult humans has taught me anything, emotional health is a significant factor in our ability to thrive as adults.

Part of raising healthy children is to equip them to be emotionally mature humans. We need to normalize mental health and emotional maturity.

No, this doesn't make children soft, weak, or snowflaky.

It makes them self-aware, compassionate, and courageous.

If our daughters develop these traits, I don't care what others want to call it.

We will know we have raised daughters who will be very capable of making their way through life with the tools of self-leadership and a strong sense of self.

Take care of your mental health.

There is nothing weak about regularly seeing a counselor. It is courageous.

There is nothing shameful about acknowledging feelings of anxiety. It is learning your body and how to take care of yourself.

What do you do when your car's check engine light comes on? You check your car's engine.

Emotions are no different.

So how are you doing?

Thank you for intentionally caring for your and your family's emotional health. Emotionally mature people are healthy people.

29
Great Catches

When we visit my parents and it rains, my mom likes to ask me if I want to go outside and play "Great Catches."

What is Great Catches?

Growing up in Travelers Rest, South Carolina, we were blessed with a yard whose spiritual gift was making puddles when it rained.

And when we had puddles in the yard, my little brother and I would get on our "catch clothes" (clothes we didn't mind ruining) and go outside. Depending on the season, we took either a football or baseball and gloves with us.

The point of the game was to see how "great" a catch we could each make into a puddle.

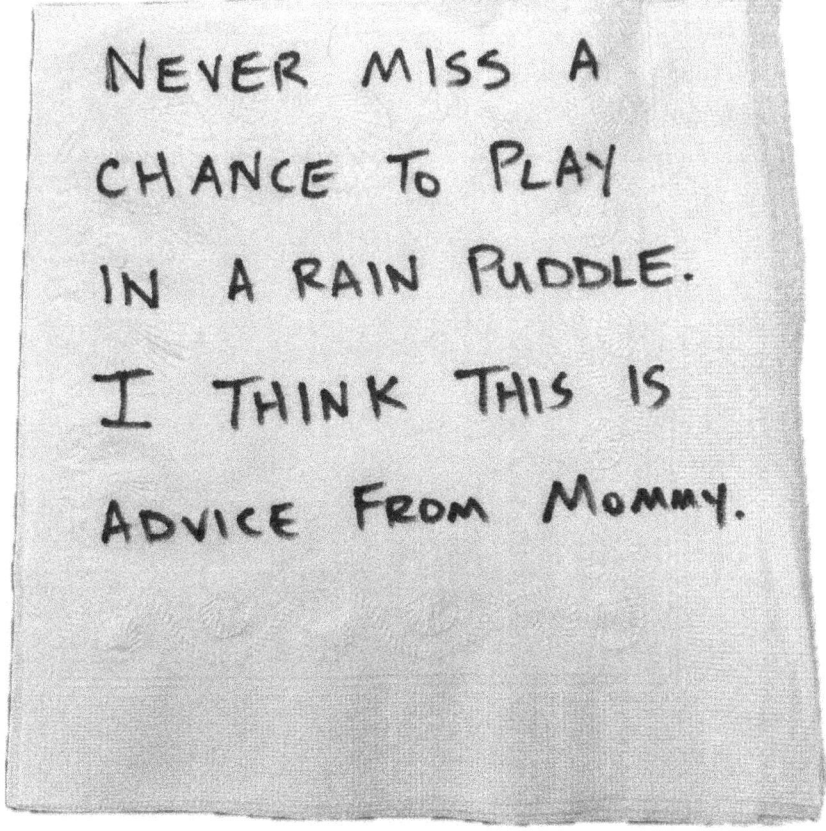

NEVER MISS A CHANCE TO PLAY IN A RAIN PUDDLE. I THINK THIS IS ADVICE FROM MOMMY.

One person would throw the ball so that the one trying to catch it would have to dive (or "layout for it," to use a "Strange" word) and stretch out as far as possible to make the catch. Then—and this is what elevated the catch to "great" or "not great"—was the combination of two factors:

1) How far would you slide on the puddle after you dove?

2) Was there an impressive amount of splash displaced from your effort?

Of course, none of that mattered if you didn't make the catch.

Now that I have a few years between me and my last Great Catch, I ponder a different idea when it rains.

At what point in life do we notice a waning of the winsome spontaneity of childhood? Especially when it rains.

My mom would also remind me of another rain-inspired lesson when I started teaching. As I moved into adulthood, she would remind me to dance in the rain. We learned this as kids playing Great Catches in the yard.

Now, as an adult, I know learning to play in the rain is also a lesson for life.

Don't let the rain keep you from joy.

Find your dancing song for the rain.

Put on your "catch clothes."

Go play in the rain.

There are moments to be created and stories to be written, even in the rain.

30
Coach

One of the people who helped shape the direction of my life was a man who entered my life in ninth grade—Coach Brian McKitrick.

Brian and his wife, Lori, moved to Travelers Rest the summer before my freshman year of high school.

I had four classes with Coach McKitrick throughout high school. He became our school's junior varsity baseball and JV basketball head coach. The place where he and I first built our relationship was on the baseball field. He was my JV baseball coach in ninth and tenth grade.

I had a solid sophomore baseball season playing JV for Coach McKitrick. However, my future as a baseball player was up in the air because of circumstances beyond my control. I was discouraged.

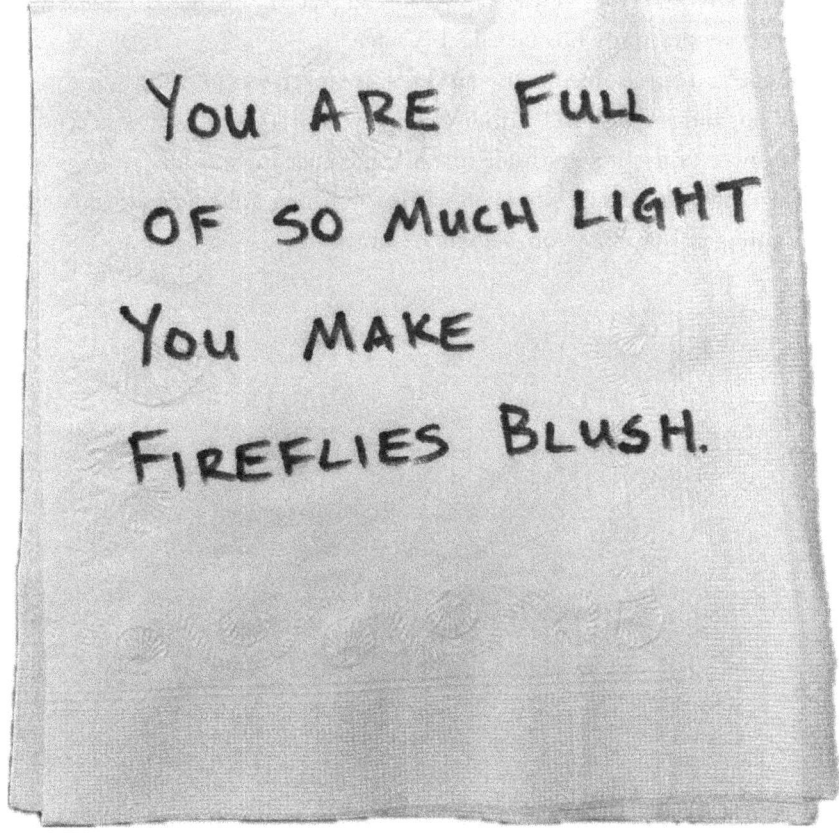

Coach McKitrick noticed my frustration.

Then he did something that changed my life.

Do you know what he did? He took me to the driving range. While we hit golf balls, we talked about baseball.

We talked about life.

He already knew me well, but when he went out of his way to take an interest in me as a human, something changed inside me.

He revealed in me something I didn't know I had.

After graduating from Clemson University, I became a high school baseball coach and teacher because of Coach McKitrick.

He was the one who stayed in my corner while I figured out what I had inside of me.

Then when I found it, he helped me light a fire that hasn't stopped burning.

And now, Coach is my guy.

Oh, and another thing you should know. If I call someone "coach" with no name after it, it means they hold a special place in my life. To this day, only two people in my life are called "Coach."

I hope you have someone in your life like Coach was and still is for me. If you do, and they are still with us, I hope you will take the time to send them a note expressing gratitude for their presence in your life.

Then, be for someone what you needed someone to be for you when you were younger. I promise you—it will be worth it.

31
Shooting Stars

We have a fun question we like to ask in my family. It goes, "Do you know who sees meteor showers?"

Our answer is, "People who set their alarm for 3:00 a.m. Choose to get out of bed at 3:00 a.m. Then go outside, in the middle of the night, and look for meteors flying through the sky."

My mom saw meteor showers. I never did. But I digress.

We often find what we are seeking.

Ever notice that when people look for someone to blame, they find someone?

Are you looking for a problem to complain about? I am sure you won't have any trouble discovering one.

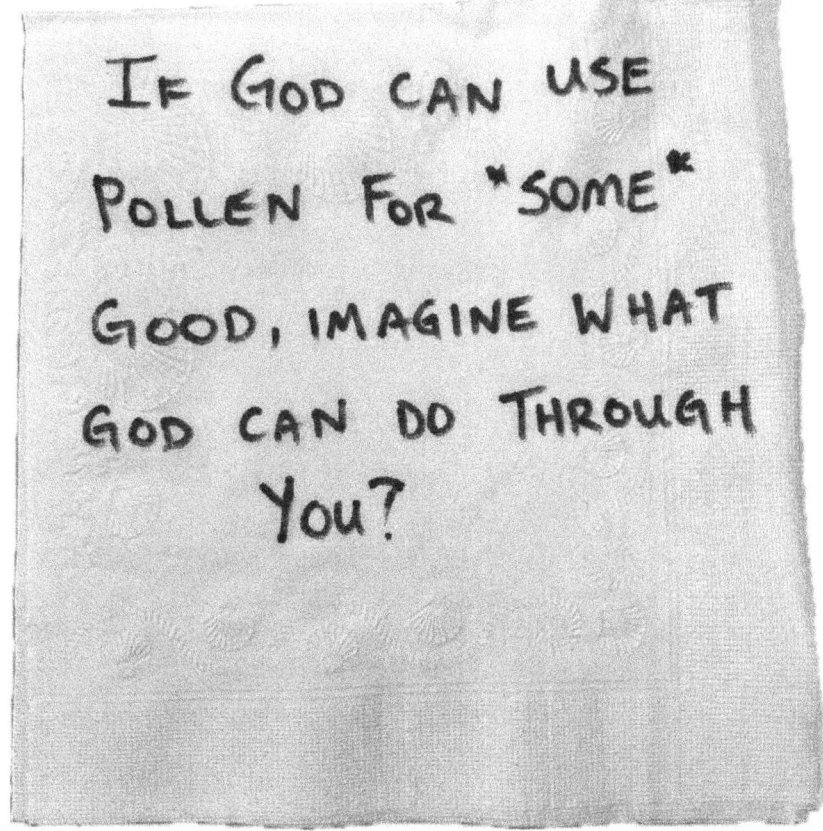

Need a good dose of cynicism today? I'm sure we know where to find a willing TV or social media personality to provoke us.

However, the flip side is also true.

If you're looking for people to encourage, you will find plenty of people who could use a gracious word today. If you are looking for opportunities to be kind to your fellow human, they are right in front of you. If you are looking for opportunities to be a part of a movement of hope in your community, they are there.

You have to be willing to look for them.

It's easy for negative and divisive ideas to dominate our culture because they often come from a place of laziness, ignorance, and a belief that people are looking for things to rally around.

Let's rally around hope.

Let's rally around encouragement and kindness.

Let's be intentional in looking for the things that can make us good and then better at being human.

Like a 3:00 a.m. meteor shower, markers of hope are all around us if we would only be willing to see them.

Where is hope blooming around you? Or better yet, who is bringing hope around you?

Can we celebrate the hope-dealers among us?

32
Four-Letter Words at Dinner

Do your kids know you are in their corner?

It's hard for me to remember what it was like to be a child sometimes. Like many of you, I remember key events and how particular experiences brought about certain emotions of joy and sadness inside of me.

However, I forgot what it was like to have my world grow each week.

Imagine, every week, you experience something new that you may or may not be prepared to process as a seven-year-old.

Remember the first time you learned not everyone went home to the same home environment you went to every afternoon?

Remember when you first learned there are certain four-letter words you shouldn't say out loud?

> LINE LEADER IS A BIG RESPONSIBILITY. YOUR LEADERSHIP IS THE DIFFERENCE BETWEEN LUNCH IN THE CAFETERIA AND LUNCH IN THE 4TH GRADE BATHROOM.
> LEAD WELL!

When I casually dropped a new four-letter word I learned at the dinner table one night in second grade, my only memory is thinking, "I didn't know my parents could hold their mouths open that long."

Or how about your first experience learning not everyone knew how to be kind to people?

I forgot there were days when your brain couldn't process all the new things you experienced as a child—when childhood innocence is introduced to the more nuanced realities of learning what it is like to be human.

Sometimes the best thing we can do for our kids is to hug them and remind them how proud we are of them at that moment.

Our days contain plenty of teachable moments. Do they also contain enough moments where you show up for your kids, and your kids experience the gift of knowing you will show up for your kids?

May we not neglect the moments where we remind our kids we are for them and in their corner as they navigate the complexities of learning to be human.

May we embrace the four-letter words that give our kids life at the dinner table. Words like love, safe, seen, hear, true, and joke.

33
It's Not Bragging—
It's Discernment

I wish more people believed in the gifts they have inside of them.

I hope you know what gifts are unique to you and that your community, and our world, needs you to let your light shine.

Without your light, there is a break in our strand of light.

And we know what happens to Christmas lights when one bulb doesn't shine.

Somewhere along the way, we were told, "Be humble and don't talk about what you are good at doing and what you can offer to your community."

First, this is a terrible misunderstanding of humility.

LIGHTNING BUGS LET THEIR LIGHT SHINE FROM THEIR BOTTOMS. IF THEY BREAK WIND DOES IT MAKE CONFETTI?

Second, can we stop being quiet about our gifts?

It's important to talk about where our strengths and passions point us.

Why? These are breadcrumbs to God's call and direction for your life.

It's not bragging to talk about your strengths and passions with people in your life.

It is called discernment.

We must get better at cultivating calling within our communities.

To downplay your gifts in the name of humility is to downplay the giver of the gifts.

Own what makes you unique. Own how God has wired you to be a part of bringing something extraordinary and redemptive into the world. Own the truth that your path and gifts are not the same as the other people in your life.

It is supposed to be this way!

Let's celebrate what God has given you that makes you unique.

34
Life Begets Life

We have to prune bushes in a garden to make space for new buds to bloom into beautiful flowers and fruit.

In life, we have to be able to end things well for new things to grow and bloom.

It's no coincidence that when I am around capable and healthy leaders, their perspectives and processes to facilitate change and foster responsible growth become apparent. They understand, as Dr. Henry Cloud writes in his book *Necessary Endings*, that "life begets life."

Cloud illustrates this point with a rose bush. He writes, "Any bush alive and thriving produces more buds every (life) cycle. And any person or business that is thriving is doing the same. Life begets life. That is normal. But it

can be too much, as well."

What does anything alive do? It creates more buds than it can sustain.

If you have been in leadership of any capacity, you understand the tension of life cycles and how "life begets life."

The ability to prune that which needs to be pruned, and to end things well, creates space and resources for new buds, new ideas, and innovation to bloom.

When we appreciate the different seasons and gifts of life cycles—jobs, social or business relationships, ideas, visions, dreams, priorities, investments, etc.—we appreciate what each season has to offer.

If we get this right, one life cycle's life, lessons, and experience will create more opportunities for life, joy, and peace as you move into the next life cycle.

Life creates more when we learn how to prune responsibly and graciously.

If you live with healthy processes, your life will create more life than you can nurture and sustain.

Celebrate! Life begets life.

35
Welcoming Jesus

I once had the opportunity to spend nine days in Israel. We walked, explored, and learned in the same places Jesus spent significant time during his adult ministry.

When you walk where Jesus walked and experience the context of his teachings in-person, you discover a connection with the character and nature of Jesus that expands the limits your belief and capacity to experience Jesus. You feel something unmistakably unique when you walk the hills of Galilee, journey the paths of the Judean wilderness, and move about the Kidron Valley.

It is one thing to learn knowledge, but wisdom occurs when knowledge engages an experience. Experiencing the context of Jesus's life in person

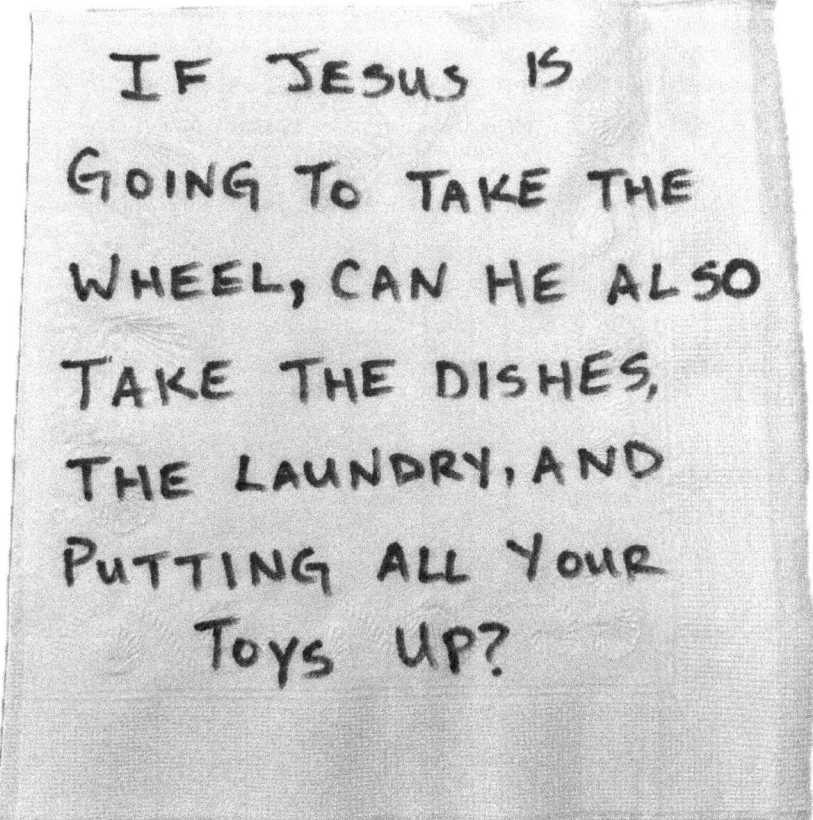

transformed how I understood and related to the Jesus we read about in scripture.

When people saw Jesus and the crowds who followed him, their reactions usually fell into two perspectives: seeing a hero or seeing the most disruptive teacher of that time.

The actions of Jesus's life inspired something intense inside people when they saw him. For most people, it was a sincere desire for hope, peace, and the expectation of healing.

Knowing Jesus wasn't simply learning about Jesus. Knowing Jesus was about knowing Jesus.

You have people like this in your life who inspire something inside of you that draws you to their spirit when they walk toward you. People who knew Jesus felt this when he approached.

"She was somebody who, when you saw her walking toward you, you couldn't help but smile."

I have heard this said about fellow clergy on more than one occasion at their funerals. What a wonderful thing to have someone say about you. People smile when they see you walking toward them. Wow!

What is it about people who, instead of wanting to be in any other place at that moment, inspire a desire inside of us to welcome them with hospitality?

Jesus had a way of inspiring a warm smile and hospitality when people saw him coming.

Who inspires you just by their presence? What is it about that person who makes you want to walk toward them rather than away from them?

In answering that question, we learn who Jesus is inviting us to become.

36
The Table

I think tables are foundational pieces of our communities.

A table is more than a piece of furniture that supports meals, books, and coffee. A table is one of the best cultivators of life and community we have as humans. Consider this: How many friendships and life-giving conversations found room to grow around a table?

Jesus was a carpenter by trade. Don't you think he knew what tables could do?

My best and most enduring friendships are that way today because we spent countless hours playing cards around a table late into the night and early into the morning in high school. Who knew we were growing roots watered with black cherry root beer and fed with breakfast from Rossie and Dave's kitchen?

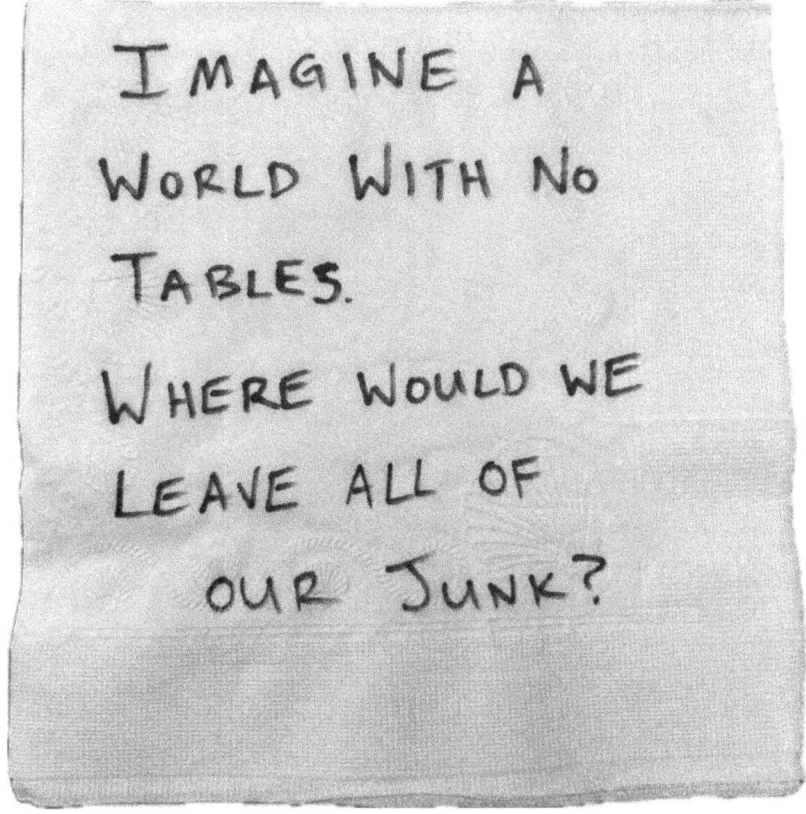

As adults, we often anchor gatherings with friends around what? A table.

Gathering around the dinner table was a pillar of the community in the early church of the first century. Throughout the pages of the New Testament, the dinner table is where relationships were formed and strengthened.

The dinner table is where life change is given a place to move about as freely and expected as we pass the salt.

Jesus's church-growth strategy was not to count worship attendance. Jesus invested in table attendance.

Throughout the Gospels, Jesus received and accepted many dinner invitations during his ministry.

Jesus would use the dinner table as a place to change things.

Following Jesus is about a way of life.

The dinner table creates space to connect the head stuff with the heart stuff and the heart stuff with the hands' stuff.

What if you pause for ten seconds every time you encounter a table today and consider the possibilities the table holds? Then, answer the invitation one table brings you today at least once.

And watch what happens.

Make the table holy again.

37
Words

I grew up navigating two speech impediments. To this day, I still live with a stutter.

Because of this, I don't take the ability to communicate for granted.

The words we use, and choose not to use, matter.

Sometimes our words precede us.

I'm aware some people have never met me in person and have formed an idea about who I am because of my napkin writings. It comes with the territory.

I don't write anything I wouldn't say to people around a table. Might I suggest the same goes for social media posts and moments where we feel a false sense of strength from degrading other humans made in the image of God?

> THERE IS A NATIONAL ALPHABET MAGNET DAY.
> TO CELEBRATE, PRETEND TODAY'S NAPKIN WAS WRITTEN WITH LETTERS ON THE FRIDGE.

The way we structure our words matters.

Donald Miller and Bob Goff taught me the word "that" weakens sentences. When we communicate, we have limited time and space to connect with our audience before they decide to keep engaging or move on.

Word efficiency and discipline are essential! (Side note: Can we agree to stop sending text messages lacking punctuation?)

Then I think about public figures.

I wish we would hold people accountable for their words in the public square. In addition, humility and learning should be encouraged, while hubris and ignorance (choosing not to see a learning moment) discredit influence.

When was the last time someone in the public square acknowledged changing their mind because they learned new facts instead of doing semantic gymnastics when a previous statement contradicted a more current idea?

Oh, you learned this statement supports your political survival better than the stance you took last year? Okay. Own it.

Words tell people if they can trust us to have integrity.

Words also let people know if they are in the presence of a fool. Mark Twain wrote, "It is better to keep one's mouth shut and be thought a fool than to open it and remove all doubt."

Our words create worlds.

The words we tell ourselves create what we believe is possible in our worlds.

The words we use can improve the world or burn it to the ground.

The words we use can build solutions, or they can multiply problems.

Our words matter.

What will you do with the words you speak, write, and share today?

38
See More People

We have an empathy problem.

Empathy is the willingness to imagine what someone else is experiencing. Then acknowledge that someone might have a different experience than you did.

And to honor the experience.

Feeling with someone else doesn't mean agreeing with their perspective. It means you made an effort to learn how they formed their viewpoint regardless of whether you agree with the view.

Andy Stanley has said numerous times, "Where you stand often has to do with where you sit."

Our experience shapes our perspective.

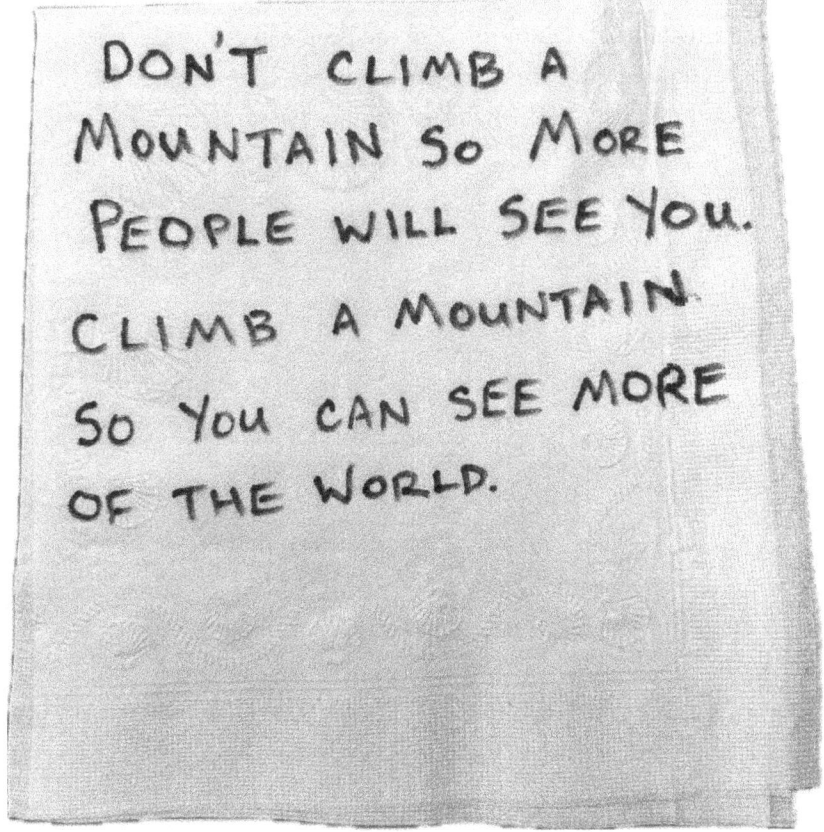

Visiting new communities and experiencing new cultures and perspectives locally, statewide, nationally, and worldwide expands my learning. Always.

It is a gift when people share their stories and experiences with me. These are chances to learn of experiences of being human from a perspective different than mine, but in a world we share.

I learn more about the world God has created when I learn more about the humans God made in God's image.

Learning other people's stories reminds me of our shared humanity.

We all want to belong to a community that sees our experience and values that experience.

We all want the opportunity to be heard in light of our experience.

But this also means we offer this to one another.

People are not problems to be solved. We are humans with a story and an experience of being human that creates a complete picture of this world God has created.

We don't climb mountains so others see more of us.

We climb mountains to see more of the people in our world.

See each other. Hear each other. Then listen to each other.

Why can't empathy be the standard and not the exception?

39
Grand-Deb and Kelly

Two people come to mind when I think about their role in helping me know what I can do. The first is Debbie Arnold, or Grand-Deb, as we now call her.

I stutter. Stuttering is frustrating. For years I felt my brain could process information faster than my mouth could communicate. I wanted my brain to slow down. At the time, it felt like an obstacle. Today, it feels like a gift.

Stuttering made it hard for me to share my voice with the world.

But God brought Debbie into my life.

In elementary school, Debbie was our school's speech therapist. I began working with her in first grade when I learned how to make Rs not sound like Ws. By the end of first grade, we resolved this speech impediment.

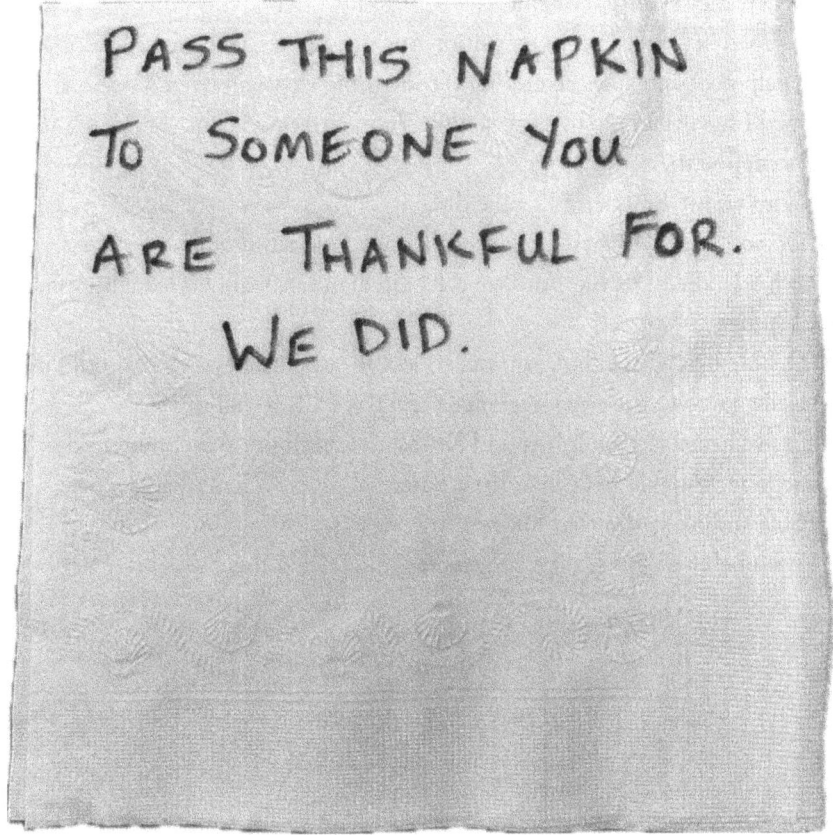

Then I started stuttering in second grade.

From second grade through college, Debbie and I continued to work together and check in on my therapy. During this time, her family became an extension of my family. We went to church together and her two daughters, Jill and Meghan, became like sisters to my brother and me. We shared Easter meals, vacations, and so many life experiences.

Believe me, speech friends, when I say you have no idea how valuable your work is. Debbie helped me find my voice.

When I went to Clemson, my public speaking class had a unit on informative speeches. I remember approaching my communications professor, Kelly Lauridsen, and lamenting how anxious I was about the assignment.

She asked me, "What is something you wish more people knew about?"

I responded, "What stuttering is really like."

Then we got to work.

One month later, my speech "Did I Stutter?" won the award for best informative speech.

When the semester concluded, I sent Kelly a thank you note.

I wrote, "I hope I am in a position one day to be a voice for stuttering and help people believe stuttering is something they can overcome. ... I learned I have it in me to show people that stuttering is not something that has to define them."

Who knew? Kelly and Debbie did.

Do you know the first person I called when I found out I won "best speech"? I called Debbie. And we celebrated and probably cried a little over the phone.

Debbie helped me find my voice. Debbie Arnold knew what I could do.

Kelly gave me the encouragement and the skills to tell my story.

I have heard Reggie Joiner and Kristen Ivy both say everybody needs somebody who will believe in their potential to live a remarkable story. Debbie and Kelly did that for me

Who believed in you at a time when you needed their belief to carry you?

40
Dreams in the Dirt

In golf, there is a saying people use to describe the process of getting better. It is, "You find it in the dirt; then you earn it in the dirt." Or, as I have written before, the way makes the way.

The same is true with our dreams. We wish for dreams to happen rather than making choices to move us closer toward a preferred vision for our life.

Dreams begin in the clouds, but they grow in the dirt.

We all have dreams that call us toward a preferred vision for our life. Yet we often hesitate or don't even give ourselves a chance to see what is possible.

How do we begin to grow our dreams in the dirt? I have some suggestions.

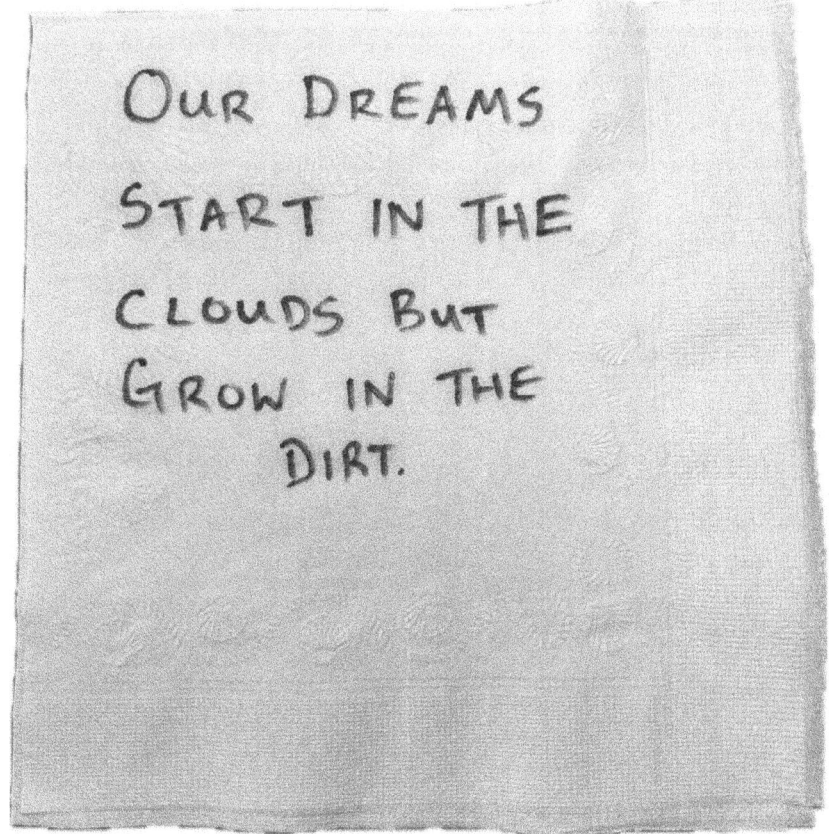

One, share your dreams with those closest to you. You will be surprised to learn the tension you feel to meet a need and the desires God placed on your heart are not limited only to your experience. Community breeds courage.

Two, take a courageous first step. The actual act of taking the first step may surprise you in the way it makes you feel. It will probably feel natural and like, "This is what I'm supposed to be doing next." The courage comes from changing the soundtrack you play in your head that tells you why you can't pursue this calling for your life. The courageous first step is also a courageous voice toward changing what you believe is true about you.

Three, commit to your process. We make hundreds of choices every day. Do the choices support the pathway we want to make for ourselves, or are we spending another day moving farther away from what God is calling us to do? It's hard to move in a direction when we aren't clear on where we are going.

Four, there is no such thing as self-made. We are all team-made. The older I get, the more I see proof of this hypothesis. You may think you are self-made, but you did not arrive at this moment alone. For better or for worse, you are the company you keep. Choose wisely. Cultivate relationships around who you want to be.

And five, do the work. There is no healthy shortcut to growth and learning.

What first step can you take to grow your dream out of the dirt today?

41
Fountains

Fountains deliver water. Drains rid spaces of water.

Jesus had something to say about the power of life-giving water.

In John 7:37-38, Jesus cried out, "Let anyone who is thirsty come to me, and let the one who believes in me drink. As the scripture has said, 'Out of the believer's heart shall flow rivers of living water.'"

The way of Jesus sounds a lot like a fountain of living water.

Yet the things Jesus calls us to—joy, peace, compassion, love, repentance, justice, and mercy—seem to have drained from the very people who claim the name of Jesus the loudest.

Please, brother and sister, can we stop draining the living waters of Christ from our communities and allowing the polluted waters of idolatry to fill

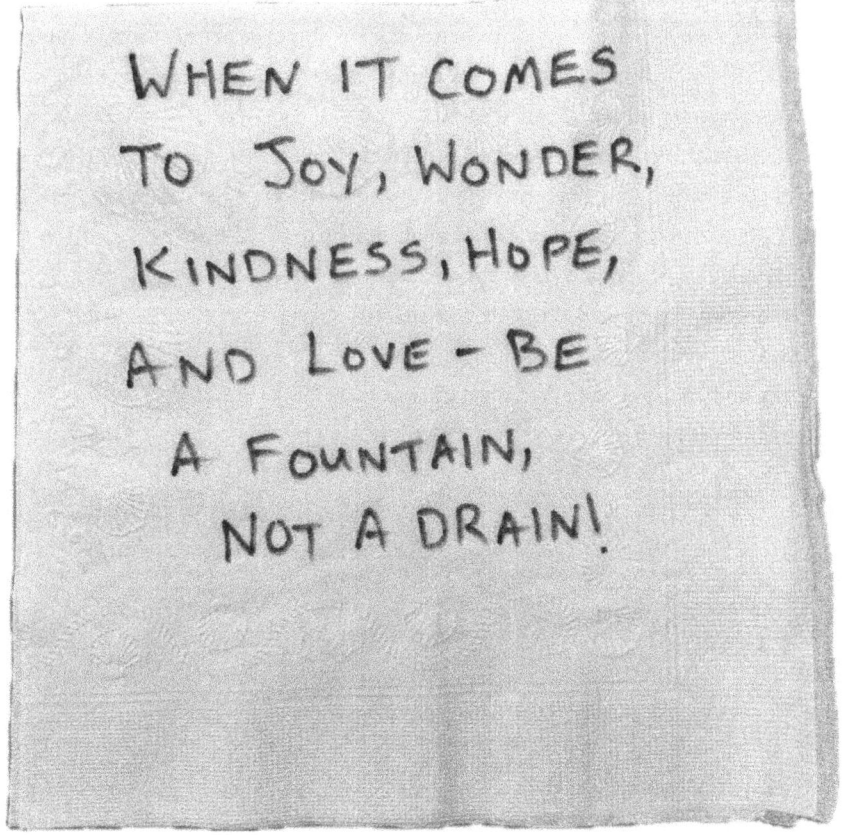

our hearts and minds instead?

Alas, there is hope.

Are we fountains of the living water of Christ, or are we draining that which is good and holy from our communities?

In a nod to the prophet Jeremiah (Jeremiah 2:13): When we are spiritually thirsty, we abandon the gifts that give life and substitute fountains of living water for cracked cisterns that hold no water.

We leak living water into the ground rather than sharing it with our communities.

Fountains move water. Cisterns store water.

Fountains keep producing. Cisterns eventually crack and leak.

Water is at its best when it is moving. In South Carolina, mosquitos show up when water collects and stops flowing. What are the characteristics of flowing water?

It moves things from old places to new places.

It can rinse and cleanse.

It can transform.

How do we rid ourselves of dependence on the cisterns of idolatry and trust our lives to the transformative living waters of God?

We cooperate with the grace of God.

To cooperate with God's grace is to drink from the streams of God's living water and to be present in such a way that our lives become fountains of God's grace, love, and mercy rather than drains that rid our communities of the very things Jesus calls us to do and be.

Are our lives giving life to our communities, or are we draining that which is good and holy?

No one runs to drains. Yet we dance in fountains.

42
Act Two

Social media makes it easy to compare our everyday journey with someone else's highlight reel. Or, in terms of telling a story, we see Act 3 while the context of Act 1 and Act 2 are left out.

The hero's journey is the standard template of stories that involve the main character, the "hero," who, because of a disruption at the end of Act 1, embarks on an adventure in Act 2.

In Act 3, the hero is victorious in a decisive crisis and returns home changed or transformed.

It's the way most writers structure stories and scripts.

When Pixar creates new movies, the hero's journey is their template. They know Act 3 isn't powerful without Act 1 and Act 2.

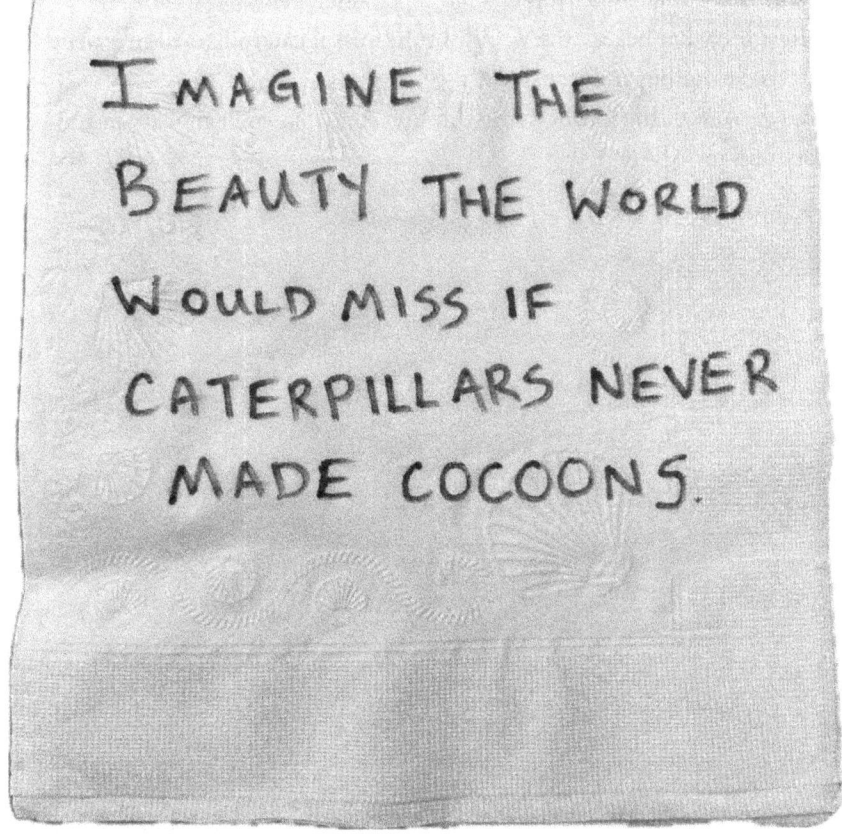

Brené Brown, in her book *Rising Strong*, describes it like this: Act 2 is the middle space. The part of the story where the main character is lost and struggling. Our lead tries to find the way forward by taking every path except the one that requires vulnerability. The struggle continues until the character realizes the only way home is through uncertainty and total vulnerability. Into the dark.

Act 2 is the messy middle. But it's where the magic happens.

Brown notes the rumble of Act 2 makes way for the reckoning and revelation of Act 3.

My faith gives me a framework to navigate when I have found myself living in an Act 2 season.

This same faith reminds me I know the direction of my story while I live and navigate the middle of my story.

Yet many never experience the presence of Christ's goodness for their life because they stay stuck in Act 2 of their faith journey.

We struggle to sit with our vulnerability and do the work to create space for our story to change. And change is possible.

Imagine what beauty the world would miss if caterpillars didn't spend seasons cocooning and transforming.

Give yourself the gift of living through Act 2, so you can walk in the peace and joy of Act 3.

43
Tell Me the Story

My oldest child enjoys hearing the story of the day she was born. I love telling her this story because, as it would happen, we ended up with the same birthday.

During Advent, and as the days move closer to Christmas Eve, there is a fun idea I kick around. This exercise imagines if Jesus would ask his parents to tell him his birth story.

Not that you need reminding, but this is Jesus.

Fully God. Fully human.

"God in a bod."

Did he know his birth story the whole time, or did he need his parents to tell him as ours did?

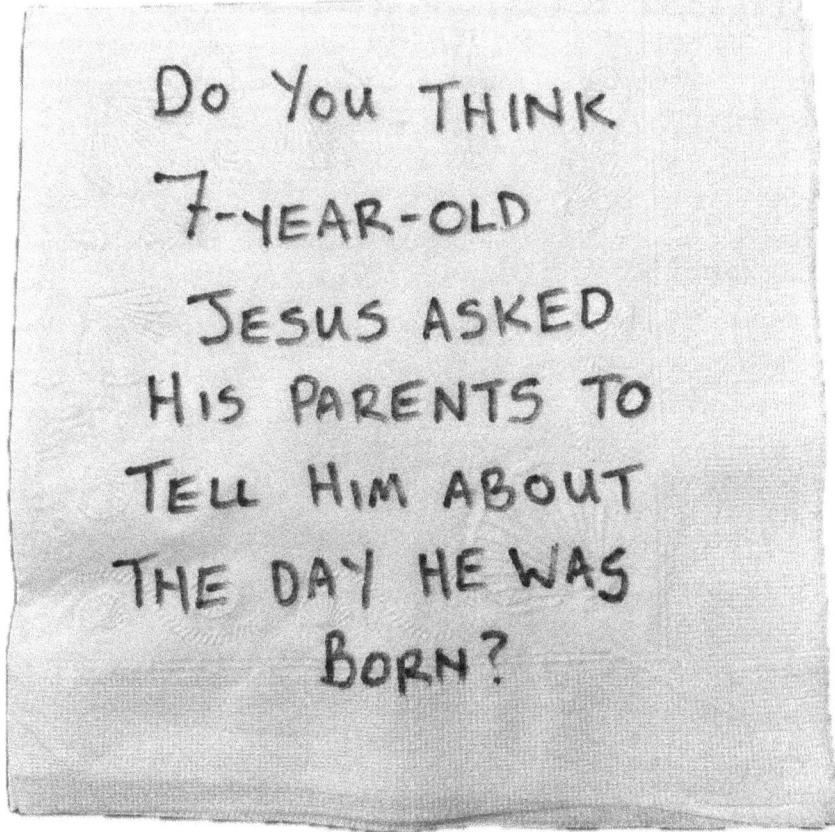

Do you think 7-year-old Jesus asked his parents to tell him about the day he was born?

Imagine a three-year-old Jesus saying, "Mommy, tell me the story again."

Smiling as she snuggles her child beside her, Mary recounts the story to a child whose eyes sparkle with curiosity and awe.

Then, as a five-year-old, would Jesus become more fascinated by hearing more about the scene than the story?

"Mommy, the innkeeper said what?"

"Daddy, make that donkey sound again!"

"How many sheep visited you after I was born?"

"Why was there a drum?"

"Did I cry?"

Did the baby who would make a way for all of humanity through a manger know he was God's gift to humanity? (Good time to remember the song started as "A Way in a Manger.")

As a pastor, each Advent I have the thrill of coming back, year after year, to the well-worn pages of Luke's and Matthew's Gospels and looking upon this beloved story with wonder and imagination.

"Tell me again, Jesus!"

Does the wonder and imagination I seek every year when I return to this story parallel the wonder and imagination young Jesus had in hearing his birth story told back to him?

"Tell me again, Mommy!"

"Tell me again, Daddy!"

Then the wise men show up with gold, frankincense, and myrrh for the baby. And I wonder, does five-year-old Jesus ask Mary, "Why did they think a baby wanted oils and gold and not a stuffed animal?"

Tell us the story again, Jesus!

44
Grief

The night before my wife was discharged after delivering our second child, we watched the movie *A Beautiful Day in the Neighborhood*.

There is a scene in the film where Mr. Rogers, played by Tom Hanks, tells a reporter facing an illness in his family, "We don't have to be afraid to talk about death. Dying is human. Being human is mentionable. If you can mention it, you can manage it."

I immediately related this to grief.

The quote steadied me and allowed me to step forward in processing everything our family experienced in the summer of 2020.

Part of being human is acknowledging the fullness of our humanity.

Experiencing excitement over things we gain and grief for things we lose.

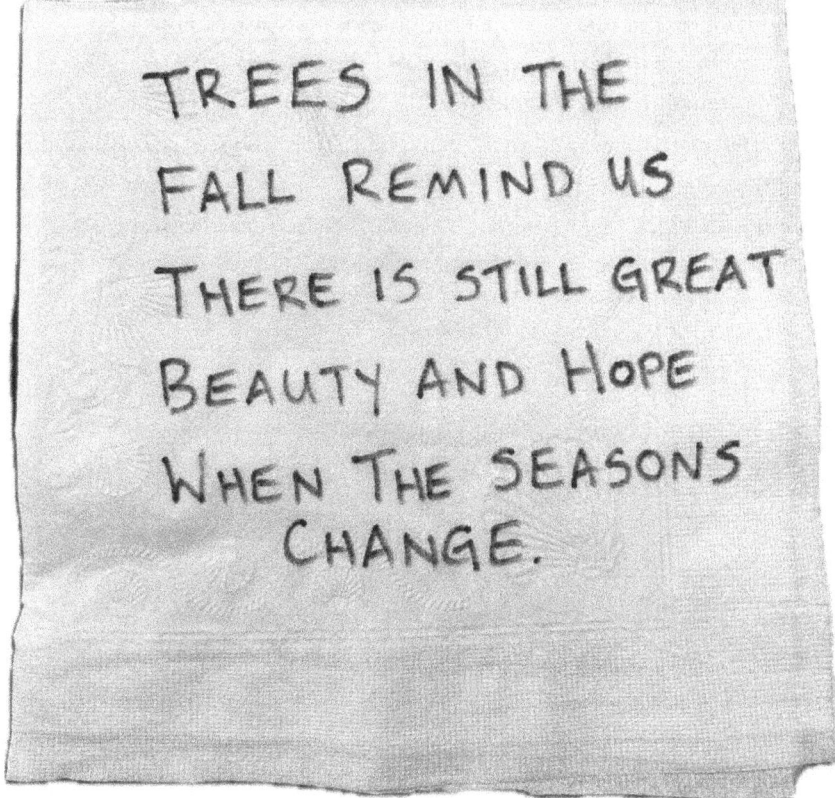

I was terrible about downplaying things I lost.

Grief isn't just about losing people.

Grief can include the loss of a job, an identity, and moments you anticipated enjoying but missed out on experiencing. I was guilty of thinking, "Oh, well, my loss isn't as bad as ...."

There is no such thing as a spectrum of grief. Grief is grief, and no grief is more intense than any other. If it's your grief, it's a big deal for you.

It's okay to acknowledge your grief.

Grief is frustrating because it does not progress in a straight line. It often feels like a circle moving us round and round.

In *A Grief Observed*, C.S. Lewis wrote, "For in grief nothing 'stays put.' One keeps on emerging from a phase, but it always recurs. Round and round. Everything repeats. Am I going in circles, or dare I hope I am on a spiral?"

Give yourself grace. You've traveled a long way between now and the beginning of your grief. You've learned a lot and grown a lot.

You've changed.

And believe it or not, this change can lead to a sense of hope.

You are human. Grief is a very human thing to experience.

Being human is mentionable.

Grief is mentionable and then manageable if we allow ourselves to talk about it.

Your grief doesn't take a backseat to anyone else's grief because your story doesn't take a backseat to anyone else's.

45
Last First Day of Third Grade

May we all embrace the invitation of starting something new.
A new grade.
A new perspective.
A new schedule.
A new career.
A new recipe.
A new secret handshake with high-fives, low-fives, fist-bumps, twirls, and sound effects.
A new friendship.
A new season of life.
Starting something new often means we are leaving something familiar.

> Congrats on your last first day of 3rd grade! May your day be filled with fist bumps, supply lists, and shoes that will never be this clean again.

There could be grief. That is okay.

There could be joy. That is also okay.

There could be grief and joy and anxiety and anticipation. All at the same time. That is also okay.

Allow yourself the grace, awe, and wonder to be present and wring everything you can out of first days, new seasons, and new spaces.

If your day is filled with high-fives and your shoes can tell a story, I'd say it was a good day.

Congrats on your last first day of today! You did it!

Acknowledgments

It's hard to fathom this labor of love is finally in your hands.

As you will read in the pages of this book, I believe no one is self-made. We are all formed by the people around us. I am fortunate to be surrounded by the best.

This begins with my wife, Lauren, from co-signing our earliest napkins to encouraging me to believe what people were telling me about the potential of this project. Lolly, I hope you know this finished product is as much your work as it is mine, for it doesn't happen without you.

Then, there are no napkins without Ava Grace! AG, I will never underestimate the power of a car ride because of you. Nor will I underestimate the possibilities of our children to bring out the best in us. I am thrilled we get to share a glimpse of the fun we have with the world. Thanks for insisting on taking your lunch all those times. I love you!

And Ellie Hope, without you, we would never have learned we could do hard things or the value of what it means to make hope our direction. I cannot wait to see what we create as you age into your "napkin years." I am convinced you will like rectangular pizza more than your sister. Good on you!

Mom and Dad, you have always supported me, even when you told me not to get the dog or buy the house. You encouraged us to take the trip, do the thing, play the song, bust out in dance, and build a life where you are willing to bet on yourself. I realize these are things I have picked up from you. I love being your son.

Writing a book built on stories from your life is easier when you have a little brother. Well, it's easier now. Thanks for being a worthy antagonist in many of my childhood memories, Trev. Perhaps I can now admit that it is a great source of pride to share a "Best Man" patch with you. In addition, thank you, Tate, for being cool with our brotherly shenanigans. Smith and Jack, I can't wait to see what stories your brotherly shenanigans will inspire in thirty years!

I come back to my belief no one is truly self-made. I can't go this far and not acknowledge my tribe. To my Arnold, Guth, and Grogg family: You are why I believe in the power of the local church and the value it brings to our lives beyond Sunday morning. It is so fun to have "sisters" who are the reason I fell in love with Clemson. And our memories. And trips. And shared experiences. Life is better with people you love. Thanks for showing me why. Besides, everyone needs a good "pea shot of a nose and into steak sauce" Easter dinner story.

Tip of the cap now to my boys, Joey and Tarik. To all my golf group texts, my United Methodist community, those in the communities I have served (Travelers Rest, Liberty, Greer, Atlanta, North Augusta, Hampton County, Aiken, Myrtle Beach, and around the country), those I have shared a table with, and those whose roots can be traced back to Travelers Rest, South Carolina. Because of you, I am not self-made. This book may have my name on it, but it has your heart within these pages.

Finally, I offer my deepest appreciation to Jessica Brodie and the *South Carolina United Methodist Advocate* team. I am proud to represent our faith community and am thankful for Jessica's leadership and skill in getting this book from a collection of napkins into what is in your hand today.

For all my people, I hope you find your stories within these pages and napkins.

Thanks for sharing your life with my life. This book is yours as much as it is mine.

About the Author

Tyler Strange was born and raised in Travelers Rest, South Carolina, and as of June 2024 resides in Myrtle Beach. He is married to Lauren, and they are raising two beautiful humans—Ava Grace and Ellie Hope—each with their own unique story to go with their names.

Tyler's story includes graduating from Clemson University with a math degree. After college, he taught high school students how and why they will use math in the future. Next, his life's journey led him to Emory University Candler School of Theology and as a campus ministry director in downtown Atlanta. After graduate school, he returned to South Carolina to serve as a pastor in the South Carolina Conference of The United Methodist Church.

His creativity, humor, and curiosity give him a unique ability to help make meaning out of life, encourage folks as they process their stories, and serve you as you discover God's preferred future for your life.

Some other things you and Tyler might talk about over a cup of coffee:

- He stutters and fully embraces this part of his story. He believes speech language pathologists are underappreciated because they literally help people find their voice.
- His family loves performing in the living room and jumping across ditches.
- His Spotify playlists range from the music of his high school homecoming dances to Lenten liturgy and everything in between.
- Tyler is curious about many things in life and loves exploring his doubts and questions, especially as it relates to his faith in God.
- Gary Player (the golf legend) once borrowed his cell phone.
- In his heart, Tyler is a coach. He was a high school baseball coach for seven years and a football coach for four years.
- He enjoys spreading hope like it's confetti and coming up with fun ways to show people they matter.
- He also loves creating new and innovative ways to use what is cultural to communicate that which is timeless.

Tyler's story has taught him hope is a direction and we make the way—one day, one story, one conversation, one breath, and one napkin at a time.

www.ingramcontent.com/pod-product-compliance
Lightning Source LLC
Chambersburg PA
CBHW070206100426
42743CB00013B/3074